Edo Japan Encounters the World

Edo Japan
Encounters the World

Conversations Between
Donald Keene and Shiba Ryotaro

Translated by
Tony Gonzalez

Japan Publishing Industry Foundation for Culture

Translation note

All Japanese names appearing in this book are given in Japanese order, with family name first. Except when fully anglicized, Japanese words are italicized and macrons are used for long vowels.

Edo Japan Encounters the World: Conversations Between Donald Keene and Shiba Ryōtarō
Donald Keene and Shiba Ryōtarō. Translated by Tony Gonzalez

Published by
Japan Publishing Industry Foundation for Culture (JPIC)
3-12-3 Kanda-Jinbocho, Chiyoda-ku, Tokyo 101-0051, Japan

First English edition: March, 2018

This book is a translation of *Sekai no naka no nihon: Jūroku seiki made sakanobotte miru* from the Collected Works of Donald Keene, Vol. 9; *Donarudo kīn chosakushū dai 9 kan sekai no naka no nihonbunka* published by Shinchosha Publishing Co., Ltd in 2013. It was originally published by CHUOKORON-SHINSHA, INC. in hardback pocket format in 1992 and as a paperback edition in 1996, and is still in print. The contents comprise three dialogues held at Hyōtei near Nanzenji-Temple, Kyoto and an unspecified location in Osaka in 1989, and at Kohōan in Daitokuji-Temple, Kyoto in 1990.

Jacket and cover design: Niizuma Hisanori, Senō Hiroya
Front and cover photo: ©Umehara Shōichi

As this book is published primarily for donation to public libraries, educational institutions, etc., commercial publication rights are available. For all enquiries regarding those rights, please contact the publisher at the following address: japanlibrary@jpic.or.jp

Printed in Japan
ISBN 978-4-86658-018-0
http://www.jpic.or.jp/japanlibrary/

Japan in the World

Japan's modern era is considered to have started in the Meiji period, the latter half of the nineteenth century. But it was the previous Edo period that made Japan's modernization possible.

The Edo period lasted for approximately 270 years, during which Japan was largely closed to the outside. Even so, the Japanese eagerly absorbed medical and scientific information leaking in from the few Dutch traders allowed to live at the Dejima trading post in Nagasaki. This was a time of rapid development for aspects of Japanese culture such as *jōruri* puppetry, kabuki theater, haiku poetry, and other forms of crafts and literature, through which Japan in turn began influencing the world, one example being the influence of ukiyo-e prints on the French impressionists.

This book presents conversations related to how Japan incorporated Western culture while developing its own in the course of modernization, presented by two eminent experts on the subject: Donald Keene, a superlative researcher of Japanese literature and culture, and Shiba, an author who has spent his career in contemplation of Japan and the Japanese. The result is keen and knowledgeable observations of the Japanese and Japanese culture stretching back to the sixteenth century, considerations that should be kept in mind as we view the Japan of today.

Uemura Yōkō
Director
Shiba Ryōtarō Memorial Museum

Preface to the English Edition

I remember my first meeting with Shiba Ryōtarō, at the time of our "dialogue" in 1971. I thought that his white hair, contrasting with his youthful face, gave him a pleasing dignity. When we spoke, his tone was friendly and (unlike many others who met me for the first time) he did not seem to worry over whether or not I would understand his Japanese.

I think I felt drawn to Shiba because he reminded me somehow of my teacher, Tsunoda Ryūsaku *sensei*. The two men did not look in the least alike, and they belonged to entirely different generations. For that matter, their interest in Japanese history and religion was by no means the same; but both men constantly searched for what was truly important, truly worth remembering in the events of history. Both men also relied on intuition when they found that the bare facts were insufficient to permit understanding. Intuition is a dangerous guide, but there are times when it is worth the risk of following it. A work dependent on intuition may be seriously flawed, but it is likely to be more interesting and perhaps more truthful than a mere accumulation of facts.

About twenty years later, the same publisher arranged for a conversation in connection with the forthcoming publication of a series of books devoted to Japan during the Edo period. When the discussion was about to start I heard Shiba say, "I don't like the Edo period."

Afterward I wondered why Shiba had spoken so harshly about the Edo period. It occurred to me that although he had written extensively about the period just before the establishment of the Tokugawa shogunate and also about the period when the shogunate was tottering and on the verge of collapse, he had not written about the more than two hundred years of Tokugawa peace. Perhaps this was because peace is less exciting to a novelist than warfare and change, but I think it was mainly because he disliked the constricted life that the Tokugawa government imposed on the Japanese people in order to preserve the stability of the regime. At our distance from Tokugawa society, we can forget its repressive nature and enjoy the haiku of Bashō, the plays of Chikamatsu, or the prints of Utamaro and Sharaku without concerning ourselves with the conditions under which those works were created. For Shiba, though, the chief characteristic of the Edo period was not its art or literature but its lack of freedom and its isolation from the rest of the world; it was a time marked by the oppression of the human spirit.

I admire Shiba's writings but he lives in my memory less as a novelist than as a wonderful human being. It is rarer to find a man like Shiba than a successful novelist. He was a good man and not merely in the conventional sense of doing no wrong. His writing inspired a whole country, not with patriotic zeal, but with a quiet awareness of what being a Japanese has meant through history.

Donald Keene
November, 2017

CONTENTS

Preface

The Joy of Conversing with Shiba Ryōtarō

Japan has always held great fascination for people throughout the world. While that fascination takes many forms, the first things that most foreigners think of when they hear "Japan" or "Japanese culture" have—with the exception of some modern industrial products—roots in Japan's early modern era, in particular the Edo period (1603–1868). This is perhaps inevitable, since Europeans learned about Japan following the arrival of the Portuguese during that time, in 1543.

The Japanese, too, got their first glimpses of the world beyond Asia in this era. Later generations of Japanese, however, have looked back on this period of history with varying sentiments. When I first arrived in Japan as an exchange student in 1953, there was a general feeling that Japan's early modern era was its absolute worst. It was seen as embodying "feudalism"—a term that at the time was considered pejorative. Youths rejected their parents' opinions as "feudalistic," and even the concepts of *giri* [duty] and *ninjō* [compassion] in Edo-period literature were derided as mere constraints on human behavior.

As a student of that literature, I found such attitudes highly regrettable. Research on early modern literature continued, of course, but some scholars spent inordinate amounts of time trying to prove that Bashō was a simple commoner rather than a samurai, while others frantically searched the works of Saikaku and Chikamatsu for attitudes of resistance to the Tokugawa regime. It takes some effort to provide an egalitarian interpretation of Bashō's haiku "Oh, how glorious! / The young leaves and budding leaves / Reflecting the sun," written at Nikko in praise of the Tokugawa clan, but it can be done. Watsuji Tetsurō's *Sakoku: Nihon no higeki* [Closed Borders: The Tragedy of Japan] (1950) is a representative critique of Japan's early modern era as a whole.

Just ten years after that book was published, however, revisionists began to present a completely different view of the Edo period. According to these scholars, Japan's isolation was no tragedy—it was instead a great boon to the nation. To bolster their claims, they cited unified praise for the shogunate from Europeans who visited Japan during the Edo period (mainly doctors posted to the Dutch merchant offices at Dejima in Nagasaki). They also presented the flourishing literature, drama, and craftwork of that time as objective support for their thesis. These were significant reevaluations, although scholars largely avoided issues like the frequent infanticides and famines. They also stopped short of calling for a return to the sort of samurai–farmer–craftsman–merchant hierarchy that prevailed in the Edo period. Still, it was a truly impressive about-face.

Value judgements aside, however, what is beyond dispute is that the early modern era was an extremely interesting time, and one that remains closely intertwined with present-day Japan in both good and bad ways. The majority of period films depict the Edo rather than the Kamakura (1185–1333) or other historical periods. While shrines and temples built in older styles are not uncommon today, most of the structures themselves date to the Edo period, and most have architectural features characteristic of that time. Japanese clothing like *haori*, *hakama*, and women's kimonos are products of the early modern era, and most traditional Japanese foods eaten today first appeared on tables then as well. Confucianism, which continues to exert a strong intellectual influence on Japanese life, also appeared at this time.

Having the opportunity to discuss this marvelous era with Shiba Ryōtarō was a great thrill for me. It goes without saying that Shiba has extensive knowledge on the subject, but, beyond that, I have great respect for the man himself. He is remarkable not only for his deep understanding of history, but also for his broad-minded attitude toward humanity.

CHAPTER 1
The Dutch Arrive

Forgotten Dejima

Shiba Holland is a relatively young country, but it has quite an impressive history. Its connection to Japan stretches back to just before the Battle of Sekigahara in 1600, when William Adams' *Liefde* drifted ashore in what was then the province of Bungo, in present-day Oita prefecture's Usuki bay. The population of Holland was around 1.5 million at the time. It's amazing that so few people were able to create the civilization that they did. The seventeenth century was a busy time for them. That's when Dutch masters like Rembrandt appeared. A busy time indeed for just 1.5 million people.

Keene In a short period of time they gained independence from Spain [de facto independence came in 1581] and started advancing overseas.

Shiba Really incredible. I have a very deep respect for the Dutch.

Keene But the Dutch today don't realize that Holland and Japan had a special relationship during the Edo period.

Shiba That's right.

Keene At least, very few do. The traditions that the Dejima trading post at Nagasaki represent have been largely forgotten.

Shiba   Japan's Hotel Okura opened a branch in Amsterdam some twenty years ago [in 1971]. They chose Amsterdam because the late president of the hotel, who's from Nagasaki, had an amazing passion for trade. He named the hotel restaurant there "Desima" and decorated it in a Dutch nautical motif. Nobody knew where the name came from. "What does 'Desima' mean?" they'd say. [Laughs] Apparently the hotel management got tired of explaining, so they changed the name.

I took a walk through the campus of Leiden University once, and asked someone how professors are addressed there. Like they do in America, they said—if you're close with a professor, it's often fine to call them by their first name. What's funny is that the professors in Japan-related fields are the exception. "They're all called 'Professor,'" I was told. [Laughs]

Apparently that's part of understanding Japan, and of teaching students the proper respect. Did the same thing happen in the Japanese department at Columbia?

Keene   Yes, I suppose the students were very polite. I spent a summer at Leiden University myself, when I was writing *The Japanese Discovery of Europe*.

Shiba   Walking around in the Netherlands provides plenty of food for thought. I think that may be particularly true for Japanese people.

When I was there, the gardens at Leiden University were being renovated. They were in the process of creating a Japanese garden. I heard they brought in someone from Kyoto University to oversee the project, and they'd already purchased some large stones. Maybe they're aiming for something like the Ryōan temple in Kyoto. I remember you telling me about a Japanese garden in Brussels, too, when you visited there for Japan Week.

Keene   Yes, there's a Japanese garden with a five-storied pagoda in it.

It was built around eighty years ago, but it had been poorly maintained, so until recently you couldn't go inside. A few years ago the Japanese government and some other groups spent a lot of money to fix it up for the Europalia festival. It's a lovely pagoda, but if you look closely there are some strange things about it. Like, stained glass with pictures of samurai and Western art.

It was raining too hard to walk around the garden when I visited, but there was an exhibition of Edo lacquerware inside the pagoda. I knew something about Muromachi (1336–1573) and Edo lacquerware, but that was the first time I had seen any from Ryūkyū [Okinawa]. That was a rare thing in the Edo period. The exhibition was from a museum collection, from Frankfurt I think it was. They were outstanding pieces, in a subdued shade of red.

Shiba   I don't think I've ever seen lacquerware from Ryūkyū. Did they have pictures on them?

Keene   Not pictures, but geometric patterns.

Shiba   Even though I use them daily, I still appreciate Japanese lacquerware. Philipp Franz von Siebold [resident physician at the Dutch trading post in Nagasaki, 1823–1829] took back quite a bit of lacquerware, but it was a very poor collection—much lower quality than I was expecting. I imagine some craftsman slapped on a single coat of lacquer and handed the pieces over to him as soon as they dried. Making really good lacquerware requires something like twenty coats. What I saw was peeling and poorly made, so it was disappointing. The curator at Holland's National Museum of Ethnology [Willem van Gulik] was the son of the diplomat and scholar Robert van Gulik (1910–1967), who was also a mystery writer. He was very earnest in his work, but still… Or maybe it's just that two months of drying followed by humidity at sea during the voyage back to Europe would have ruined even the best lacquerware.

Keene   I don't think high humidity would be a problem, but drying is hard on lacquerware. Siebold presumably brought back items that he felt had some kind of research value or exceptional artistry, but they weren't of particular interest to the Dutch until twenty or thirty years ago. No doubt they were left in a basement somewhere, forgotten. Even if they looked great when they first arrived in Holland, leaving them in a dry room for a century would surely damage them.

Europeans loved Japanese lacquerware, which they called "japan." You don't hear it called that much anymore, but for a long time "japan" meant lacquerware, just like "china" can mean ceramics. Both were curiosities for Europeans, and both could be incorporated into daily life. There were other wonderful things in Japan—images of the Buddha and the like—but Europeans couldn't tie them to daily activity. They embraced ceramics, porcelain, and lacquerware right away, though. Those items were made in huge quantities in Japan and China and exported to Europe in the eighteenth and nineteenth centuries, so you'll sometimes see old Japanese pieces even in rural European towns. I've been shown items like that several times. An acquaintance of mine lives in France near the Belgian border, and he often finds curious Japanese pieces in rural France.

Shiba   There's a port town north of Amsterdam called Hoorn where ships returning from Japan used to drop anchor to rest for a night and sell a few goods before arriving in Amsterdam the following day. That made it a magnet for nobility and wealthy families throughout Europe. I heard that one German noble ran out of money there when he overbid on Japanese goods, and to make up the difference he sold some of the troops he'd brought along. [Laughs]

In any case, products from Japan were just curiosities. With the possible exception of ukiyo-e woodblock prints, they didn't alter the life and culture of Europe.

Keene   I'm not sure what kind of porcelain Europeans had before Imari ware arrived. Actually, I think most Europeans were eating their meals off of wooden or metal plates before that. Whatever ceramics they had probably had pretty pictures, but I don't think the ceramics themselves were of very high quality.

So when Japanese ceramics arrived in Europe, I do think it had a large effect on the lifestyles of the wealthy. There were probably hygiene benefits as well. Ceramics and porcelain can be easily cleaned by washing, but wooden items are full of crevices that bacteria can hide in. That can cause all kinds of disease. In ways like this, I think the introduction of everyday items from Japan greatly improved the lives of Europeans.

Shiba   The porcelain in Japan was that Chinese type developed in the mid-fourteenth century, between the end of the Yuan dynasty and the beginning of the Ming. It had that lovely cobalt blue coloring like diluted ink, and in Japan it was called *gosu* or *sometsuke*. It came to define the color of ceramics used in daily life, and of porcelain in particular.

It seems that Europeans took quite a liking to that porcelain as well. When I took a Lisbon-bound express train from Madrid to Portugal—a train that happened to be built by the Italian company Fiat—all the Portuguese stations were decorated with tiles showing lovely landscapes. The illustrations were done in the same cobalt blue, so I got the impression that Europeans, and especially the Portuguese, really like that color.

Keene   There's a similar tradition in the Netherlands. Dutch tiles, especially those from the seventeenth century, are cobalt blue.

Shiba   I wonder if that was considered an exotic color in those days.

Keene   Earlier European ceramics used gaudier colors. They were red and green and yellow, especially the Italian majolica, and the illustrations were usually of human figures. Japanese ceramics, in contrast, had natural scenery and flowers, which Europeans found very attractive.

All Portuguese churches were beautifully tiled, both inside and out.

Shiba   So you noticed the tiles too. I really loved the ones in the train stations. I'd like to get back for another look.

Keene   Yes, I was quite taken by them. Most Japanese probably aren't aware of it, but I think Japanese products, and ceramics in particular, greatly changed European lifestyles. The museums there still have many old pieces of Imari ware—Arita ware, really—and similar pieces. Just five or six years ago, a sunken Dutch ship filled with ceramics was found off the coast of Sumatra. The ceramics weren't particularly beautiful, but they fetched quite a price at auction in Amsterdam just because they were unquestionably from the eighteenth century. I really wanted at least one piece, of anything really. I tried ordering a teacup for 800 guilders, but I wasn't able to get anything for that price.

Shiba   Well that's a shame. 800 guilders? I think one guilder is around 70 yen, so what does that work out to? Anyway, even that wasn't enough?

Keene   It wasn't, no. Every piece was priced above that. These were just ordinary items for the Japanese, not particularly attractive, but the Europeans really wanted them—and still do.

I recently saw a mural in Italy that depicted a wedding scene with something like crockery, but it was all made of metal. This was from the sixteenth century, before ceramics had started to develop much.

The Pros and Cons of "Isolation"

Shiba   Talking about guilders reminds me of the streets in Leiden, which are paved with fist-sized cobblestones that were laid down around 1600. There are no mountains in the Netherlands, so they must have been bought from somewhere. I asked someone who knew about such things how much a stone like that might have cost in the seventeenth century. "In the 1600s, they cost one guilder each. They still do," he said. [Laughs] Can you imagine going all the way to the mountains of Switzerland or Germany just to buy rocks to walk on? That must have been rough.

Keene   Speaking of the lack of mountains in Holland, in 1690 there was a German doctor named Kaempfer at Dejima who, when asked what country he was from [because only Dutch nationals were allowed into Japan], said he was from the "Dutch mountains." [Laughs]

Shiba   Apparently he had a strange Dutch accent that the Japanese translators couldn't quite place.

Keene   It must have been quite strange indeed.

Shiba   There's a place in southern Holland that locals call a "mountain," but it's actually just a hill around one hundred meters high. I've never been there myself, but I hear that Americans and British who visit laugh and say, "That's no mountain!" I guess it's the closest thing the Dutch have.

Keene   When the first Dutch arrived in Japan, they must have thought the place was nothing but mountains, compared to their own country.

Shiba   Siebold was in a similar situation to Kaempfer, both being German. I wonder if there are any legends about him being told to claim that he spoke Mountain Dutch if anyone from the Japanese government questioned his accent.

Keene   Siebold probably read Kaempfer's *History of Japan*. Recently, a German scholar teaching in Australia read a 1727 English translation of Kaempfer's book, and found that it was filled with errors. When she read Kaempfer's original work, it was clear that he was far more impressed with Japan than what the translation implied. The Swiss person who translated it hadn't wanted to anger Europeans, so he qualified a lot of what Kaempfer had written, for example making it sound like he hated Buddhism. The scholar is working on a new English translation now[1], which I'm sure will lead to new interpretations of Kaempfer's work.

Shiba   I'll look forward to that.

Keene   Yes, I'm sure he had high praise for Japan. Of course, he does even in the translation we've had until now, but we don't know what parts the translator changed. The Japanese are most interested in the appendix, which was translated into Japanese by Shizuki Tadao (1760–1806) in 1801 under the title *Sakoku-ron* [Isolationist Theory]. I don't remember what the original German term was, but it was translated as *sakoku*. It was a newly coined word that hadn't existed in Japanese up to that point. I don't think the Japanese realized that they were living in an isolated country until *Isolationist Theory* was translated.

In contrast to prevailing opinion today, Kaempfer thought that isolationist policies were a wonderful thing. Other Europeans probably considered isolationism a barrier to free trade, or a disagreeable policy that prevented free entry into Japan, but Kaempfer wrote that the Japanese lacked nothing, and since they already had everything they need, why open up?

The thing he envied most was that there was no war in Japan. That was huge. There were wars everywhere in seventeenth-century Europe, so many that people would forget what they were fighting over. The Thirty Years' War had ended just a few decades earlier, and Kaempfer couldn't have left Nagasaki to return home even if he had wanted to, because Germany was in a war that prevented him from reaching it.

Directors of the Dutch trading post continued complaining until many years later that they were only being sent goods that the Japanese

1. Bodart-Bailey, B. (1999). *Kaempfer's Japan: Tokugawa Culture Observed*. University of Hawaii Press.

had no need for—exotic birds and animals, new textiles and the like. They said trading like that could only hurt Japan. Of course, the Japanese gained from trade at Nagasaki in other ways. If nothing else, they were able to hear about what was going on in Europe from the Dutch who were stationed there.

The question of whether isolation helped Japan or hurt it was a matter of concern back then, and it still is. Isolationism kept foreign influences from directly entering Japan, and it also prevented wars. Thanks to that, Japan was able to develop in unique ways. For instance, a form of comic linked verse called *renku* had emerged much earlier, but only in the early modern period did Bashō (1644–1694) and others develop it into the more artistic haiku. Kabuki, too, developed from the theater of Izumo no Okuni with little foreign influence, as did *jōruri* sung narratives.

Of course, isolationism had its downsides. Worst of all was that while I believe Japan's culture was more advanced than that of the West during the Muromachi (1336–1573) and Momoyama (1573–1600) periods, that didn't continue. The Japanese got news that an industrial revolution was taking place in the West, and that the natural sciences were advancing. They would hear that, say, a new planet had been discovered, but there were no telescopes in Japan, so they couldn't make discoveries like that on their own.

Astronomy may not be the most practical of sciences, but the same thing was happening in other academic fields. The Japanese knew about this because of publications like *Oranda fūsetsugaki* [Dutch Reporting of World News], but they weren't able to actually engage in, say, medical research until Siebold and others started teaching them medicine in the late Edo period. With no industrial revolution, Japan was unable to compete with other countries. That led to a lot of suffering until the country opened up at the start of the Meiji period (1868–1912). So isolationism was bad for Japan in those ways, but I'm not sure how to determine whether it was a good thing or a bad thing overall.

Shiba   I'm not sure either. It's quite difficult to establish a thesis one way or the other, to point to a process that occurred over the course of 270 years and say whether it was good or bad.

Here's an example. Dutch trading vessels arrived at Nagasaki after a long voyage, carrying various tools. You mentioned telescopes a minute ago, how there were none in Japan. The Dutch didn't bring telescopes, but the sailors at least had double-magnification spyglasses—finely made, heavy brass equipment. The Japanese saw those and crafted something similar using highly decorated rolls of lacquered papier-mâché. They could be extended and collapsed just like the Dutch ones, and they were even waterproof. So not only did they work just as well, but they were lighter, and even more beautiful.

That's a good example of the difference between a country that's isolated and one that isn't. If Japan hadn't been closed, I imagine the Japanese might have learned brass-working and made their own spyglasses, but since it was closed, they instead made something entirely their own, something even more beautiful. That's the culture of an isolated country.

The Dutch did strongly influence Japan, but they couldn't teach the Japanese anything about the industrial revolution, which was so very important. Understanding the industrial revolution wasn't something you could do from afar, by reading a textbook or whatever—Japanese people had to visit Europe and experience it for themselves. Also, if an industrial revolution had occurred in a domain like Satsuma or Tsugaru, the shogunate would have fallen apart right away. So isolationism had a self-preserving function. That's why it continued for 270 years. Of course, in the end the greatest benefit of isolationism was that it prevented wars, not that it helped the shogunate.

I heard there was recently a speech at an ecology conference in Rome where the speaker talked about how wonderful the Edo period was. But since Japan was closed at the time, I don't know how many relevant lessons other countries can draw from that period. The Edo period certainly doesn't provide a good model for Iran, or for Lebanon. What kind of domestic support would an Iranian get by saying "We should close the borders and cease all conflict. We should focus only on pre-

serving Iranian culture"? So saying that the Edo period was good because of its isolationism doesn't provide any useful lesson to the countries of the world. The Japanese do get to talk about the beautiful
papier-mâché telescopes they made, though.

The big Dutch ships used ropes to hoist their sails, and that requires
pulleys, right? People in Edo Japan saw those pulleys and thought they
were great, so they added them to their single-sailed ships. So their sails
became a little easier to hoist, but that's about it, at least as far as sail-
boats go.

Around the time of Ieyasu, the first Tokugawa shogun, boats were
only allowed to have one sail—although it wasn't written down as an
actual law or anything. The government felt uneasy about boats being
able to go too far. Not only could boats with several large sails travel
to far-off locations, they could also leave from Ise—what's now Mie
prefecture—to launch a direct attack on Edo castle. That of course
wasn't in the shogunate's interest, so boats were limited to a single
sail.

Ships in the earlier Muromachi period actually had more sails. Ships
also had many sails during the Warring States period [1467–1603],
modeled after Western ships. But Edo-period ships only had a single
sail, except toward the end when a small secondary sail was sometimes
permitted, as an exception. When Admiral Perry entered Edo bay and
saw those ships, he knew they didn't amount to much—a design like
that makes boats catch so much wind they easily capsize. As a sailor
himself, I'm sure he felt sorry for Japanese crews.

That's another aspect of isolationism. You have to wonder how many
sailors died during the 270 years of the Edo period as a result of those
policies. If we had data like that, I'm sure we'd see numbers of people
suffering in Japan that far outstripped Europe. I mean, consider the
number of boats that were travelling along Japan's coasts back then,
given its bustling product-based economy. All of them were dangerous
single-sailed craft. So isolationism surely wasn't to the benefit of the
crews aboard those boats.

But again, these are just the pros and cons for one segment of the population. They don't really address the overall picture.

Keene   That reminds me of another peculiar feature of the Edo period that doesn't really have a parallel in any other country. Namely, guns.

There were gun corps in Oda Nobunaga's time, and the Japanese weren't just using them, either—they were manufacturing their own high-performance guns. But they gave them up. Not completely—hunters still used them—but the military abandoned them. No other country has ever stopped using guns once it had them. But the shogunate decided that the guns would be put away, and swords used instead. That is a very rare phenomenon.

Shiba   It is indeed. During the Edo period, limits were placed on the number of guns daimyo were allowed to produce, and guns had to be so highly decorated they were more like works of art.

Keene   Just like Japanese telescopes, which ended up as better pieces of art than tools for looking at stars. There's an illustration in Ihara Saikaku's (1642–1693) *Life of an Amorous Man* that shows its protagonist Yonosuke using a spyglass to watch a woman bathe. So that's part of the aesthetic.

Shiba   Going all the way back to the Nara period (710–794), Japanese culture didn't have much use for stars. Japan has never been very interested in the stars, maybe because the skies are too cloudy.

Keene   Hirata Atsutane (1776–1843) wrote somewhere that when he was asked why the stars are never mentioned in the *Kojiki* [Records of Ancient Matters], he replied, "That's the stars' fault." [Laughs]

Shiba   Yeah, there's not much. The only originally Japanese astronomical name I can think of is *subaru* [the Pleiades]. All the others use Chinese loan words. You'd think more would have native names.

Even if you can't see the stars well in Japan on most nights, that isn't the case *every* night, so you have to wonder why people didn't take a greater interest in them. I think it's because people in places like the Middle East used the stars for navigation. Islamic culture spread during the Crusades of the eleventh and twelfth centuries, so there was a solid cultural base for stargazing in Europe. Europeans have been interested in the stars for a very long time, probably because they are helpful in maritime navigation. For example, in the time of Portugal's Prince Henry the Navigator (1394–1460), people knew they could use them to tell where their boat was during long sea voyages. But in Japan the stars didn't have that kind of connection with daily life or nautical techniques, so it seems people never thought to relate them to beauty.

Keene Right. Stars don't show up in Japanese art very much. No Japanese poet ever wrote a line like "my lover's eyes shine like the stars."

Shiba Yeah, there aren't many expressions in Japanese that compare things to stars. We say "like the stars" to refer to a large number of prominent figures gathered in one place, but that's all I can think of. But Westerners have made the stars into both literary objects and objects for practical use.

The Edo shogunate created the post of official astronomer when it realized the Japanese calendar was drifting and needed to be updated. The first appointment, in 1684, went to Shibukawa Shunkai (1639–1715; a.k.a. Yasui Santetsu II), a go player who also studied astronomy and calendars. His position became a permanent post responsible for matters related to astronomy, the calendar, measurements, and cartography. The Meiji-period literary figure Yamaji Aizan (1865–1917) was born into the Asakusa family that traditionally held the position of official astronomer. But that's about the extent of Japan's cultural connection with the stars.

Keene Maybe that's why the Japanese did not resist the concept of heliocentrism when they first heard about it from Europeans. The first

Europeans who supported it were killed for their belief.

Shiba   Well that was because of Christianity, which wasn't an issue in Japan. Here, it was probably just a one-minute conversation. "The earth moves around the sun." "Oh yeah? Interesting." [Laughs]

Keene   Or maybe because Amaterasu is a sun goddess, being in the center is her rightful place.

Shiba   You may be right. The Japanese worshipped the sun, just like all cultures have at some point.

The Desire for Knowledge amidst Isolationism

Shiba   The word "isolationism" first appeared in the late Edo period, but when Perry came and pressed Japan to open its borders, groups who were opposed to doing so apparently thought Japan had been an isolated country since its earliest days. People back then knew a lot about Chinese history, but little of their own beyond Rai San'yō's (1781–1832) *Nihon gaishi* [An Unofficial History of Japan], and he didn't use the word "isolationism."

Keene   It's surprisingly easy to create traditions. It seems as if by the late Edo period the Japanese had forgotten just how many Portuguese had come to Japan, and how many Japanese had gone overseas during the Momoyama period.

Shiba   They had indeed.

Keene   In the late Edo period, Westerners thought isolationism was just a word. The law said Europeans had to stay in Dejima, but actually there were people like Siebold who had their own clinics and so on in Nagasaki, so no one thought Japan's "isolationism" meant much. But when Takahashi Kageyasu (1785–1829) gave Siebold a detailed map of Japan created by Inō Tadataka (1745–1818), Takahashi was arrested and later died in jail, and Siebold was banished. That must have made the point, and the system became impossible to ignore.

Shiba   There were only ten or eleven Dutch at Dejima, maybe a few more if you include household staff, and as a rule they couldn't leave the island, not even for a stroll around town. Siebold was allowed to create a school in Nagasaki as a special exception. But even so, I think the effect of the Dutch on Japan starting in the mid-Edo period was one of the greatest events in human history. I mean, how was it possible for just a dozen or so people at one location to have such a huge impact on a society?

If Japan had been a Dutch colony, then of course it would have been strongly influenced by Holland and the rest of Europe. But in this case it was the isolationist Japanese who approached the Dutch, out of curiosity. A curiosity born of isolationism, I suppose.

Keene   I don't think that's all there is to it. The Japanese have always had a strong interest in other countries. China at first, but then later on the rest of the world. Japan was about as far as you could get from Europe, and its isolationism prevented travel abroad, but the Japanese knew more about Europe than people in the nearby Middle East did. There were Arabs in northern Africa living within sight of Spain, and Europe was visible from Turkey as well, but no one in those areas had much interest in Europe, so they didn't study it. But the Japanese had a very keen interest in Europe. Not necessarily for any practical purpose or financial benefit, just because they wanted knowledge for knowledge's sake.

Shiba   Yes, a pure desire for knowledge. I think that's a wonderful thing. You know those pinhole cameras we used to make, a box with a tiny hole that makes an exposure on photosensitive paper? Well, Dejima was just like that pinhole.

You mentioned the Arabs a minute ago. I think that they have an inward ideology. I think the Japanese have the opposite, an outward ideology. We tend to think that novel ideas don't arise on these islands, that they come from other places—first from China, then from Holland and so on. It was those eleven Dutch at Dejima who showed us that Europe had something that we didn't have, something beyond Chinese philosophy and government and science—if you can call it science, science in the Joseph Needham sense, at least.

Nowadays, we Japanese have finally realized that it's time for us to create our own ideologies, but new thought doesn't arise easily in such a monoculture. It seems to require cultural diversity.

Keene   Or it could be the opposite, that Japan had too many ideologies. I don't know very much about Southeast Asia, but it's possible that Japan wouldn't have developed like it did if it had been strictly Buddhist like many of those countries. Or if it had been strictly Confucian like China, it may have remained satisfied with its own culture. If Japan had only had Shintō, it may have come to consider itself the one true holy land. But having all three forced Japan to recognize each—the same people believed in both Buddhism and Shintō, and studied Confucianism. Once you have three ideologies, it's not so hard to add a fourth and a fifth. If you're locked into one ideology, the tendency is to reject all others. Since Japan had three, it was okay for Western thought to come in, and Christianity. There was room for other ideas.

It's extremely hard to determine if Japan ever had a predominant ideology, because Japan is such a rare case in world history. Many great Japanese thinkers accumulated a broad range of thought. No matter how fervent a Buddhist you were, you couldn't have been ignorant of Confucianism, nor could you have ignored Shintō. Even staunch proponents of Shintō like Hirata Atsutane had an interest in Western studies and thought it important to incorporate newly learned natural sciences, and to study other newly introduced ideas. There was no rejection of those.

Japan's isolationism made learning about other countries very difficult, but people wanted that knowledge, and no religion prohibited its acquisition, so anything could be studied. Other countries banned the study of certain subjects for religious reasons, as happened with heliocentrism in Europe.

Shiba Unlike most modern people, the sinologist Yoshikawa Kōjirō (1904–1980) was very conscious of Confucianism. He wanted to live a purely Confucian life, and hated Buddhism because he believed it stood in opposition to Confucianism. But when I attended his funeral, it was a Buddhist ceremony. [Laughs] Jōdo Shinshū sect, in fact.

Keene That's the way it goes. I'm sure the nativist scholar Motoori Norinaga (1730–1801) followed Jōdo too.

Shiba No doubt he did. Perhaps he too was a man of many ideologies. I know of only one person who had a Confucian funeral in the Edo period—Yamazaki Ansai (1619–1682). Funerals were considered best left to monks, and only Ansai was peculiar enough to want something different.

Keene Both then and now, Japanese apply ideologies according to need. Buddhist wedding ceremonies are very rare, for example. Wedding ceremonies are usually Shintō, funerals are Buddhist, and daily life is Confucian. Meanwhile, academic life is based on Western science and ideologies.

CHAPTER 2
Japanese Views of the Early Modern Era

The Era When "Traditions" Were Created

Shiba As you say, weddings are Shintō ceremonies, which shows that traditions can develop in just a few decades. I think it was only in the Taishō period (1912–1926) that Shintō priests first started conducting wedding ceremonies at shrines. They apparently got the idea from watching Christian ceremonies, and figured they should do something similar. Poof, a new tradition. Before that—in the Edo period of course, and even until recently for some old families—wedding ceremonies were held at the groom's home. There was nothing religious about it and no priest in attendance, just a ceremonial sipping of rice wine, which is purely secular. If you held a wedding ceremony without a Shintō priest today, conservative guests would probably complain that you were going against Japanese traditions, but in truth those traditions only go back around seventy or eighty years.

The tradition of girls learning tea ceremony as a form of refinement is new, too, the result of the Urasenke school of tea ceremony teaming up with women's magazines in the Taishō era to promote the idea. Before that, tea ceremony was something men did! [Laughs] I'm sure there are plenty of other "traditions" out there with similar back-stories.

Keene Most Japanese traditions practiced today were formed in the Edo period. The temples we have now are from that time. A few older ones are scattered here and there, but if you want to worship at a temple from the Kamakura period, you'll probably have to visit Kyoto. And if you go to a more modern temple, one built after the Edo period, you'll probably feel like you're missing something. There's just this general feeling that one should worship before a Buddha in an Edo-period temple, because that's the Japanese tradition.

The food that we consider traditional is also from the Edo period. Few people even stop to consider what the Japanese ate before that. They loved wine in the late Muromachi and early Edo periods, and Toyotomi Hideyoshi (1537–1598) ate beef stew. This idea that the Japanese don't eat much meat and don't drink Western-style wine is an Edo concept. Go back to the Heian period (794–1185), and the Japanese even ate cheese.

Clothing is the same way. Back in the Muromachi or Momoyama periods, women didn't wear the kimonos you see today. But from the early Edo period through to today, they've basically been the same, with some minor variation. Japanese-style houses and the use of tatami mats originated then as well. So the food is Edo, the clothing is Edo… All of these traditions are from the Edo period.

Many Westerners form their impressions of Japan through its art, specifically through works by Andō Hiroshige (1797–1858), Katsushika Hokusai (1760–1849), and similar artists. Specifically, it's the art and theater of the Edo period, not the older *emaki* scroll-works like *The Tale of Genji*, that people consider to be "Japanese." *The Forty-seven Ronin* has been widely read in the West, and translations have been available since the early Meiji period, so many Westerners get their ideas of Japanese sense from that work. So in various ways, the image of "traditional Japan" stems from the Edo period for non-Japanese as well. Today I suppose there's also a strong image of the Japanese salaryman, but most Westerners know little about what occurred before the early modern age, and contemporary aspects of Japanese culture are so influenced by the West that they have little appeal overseas.

Shiba At the start of the Meiji period, public servants were ordered to wear Western clothing, but from what I understand Westerners thought Japanese men in suits looked silly. Ōyama Iwao (1842–1916) is always depicted in Western clothing or a military uniform, but apparently some Westerners thought he looked very strange. I think it was Edward Morse (1838–1925), discoverer of the Ōmori shell mound, who was once invited to the Rokumeikan hall to meet Ōyama. On that day Ōyama was dressed in samurai garb, which for him was just a costume, but Morse was deeply impressed, and thought he looked magnificent. So when Japanese wear the clothing that they developed in the Edo period as best suited to their bodies, Westerners think they look great.

When Westerners think of Japanese, in the extreme case they seem to think that Edo-period fashions are still around, that men still wear topknots or whatever. Or at least there's some part of them that thinks the Japanese look better in Edo-period clothing than in Western clothing. I think people throughout the world have a good idea of what the Japanese wear today. They've seen salarymen, after all, but I can't help but wonder if, when they see those salarymen, they don't tend to imagine them with topknots. Not in a bad way, mind you, but with affection.

Keene Speaking of the Rokumeikan, the whole point of that building was to show Westerners that the Japanese were cultured, too. That they could use knives and forks to eat, that they could dance in Western clothing, things like that. But in the end it had the opposite effect. Specifically, this is when Japan first started developing a reputation as a copycat nation. Nobody had said anything like that until then, but the image of Japanese people in Western dress mimicking Western dance was a source of mirth.

I suppose that shouldn't be surprising. Westerners had lived their entire lives in Western clothing, so when adult Japanese try to put on these strange outfits and perform unfamiliar dances, well, of course that won't go well. That reputation of the Japanese as copycats lasted until very recently. When I first got into teaching, just after the Second World War, almost everyone in the UK had that impression. I don't think people think that today, though…

Shiba All because of the Rokumeikan, back in the Meiji period.

Keene Westerners visiting Japan in the late Edo period never said things like that, and when Japanese delegations travelled overseas, everyone was impressed by how fine they looked. I guess they just needed a little practice in wearing Western clothing.

Shiba They just didn't get it. Unfortunately, I often wonder if we still haven't.

Positives and Negatives

Keene In the Meiji period, people saw the shogunate days in a bad light. Anything related to the Tokugawa shogunate in particular was bad. For example, since noh drama had always been seen as entertainment for the shogun, most noh actors found themselves unemployed in the early Meiji period. They ended up abandoning their profession to become farmers and policemen and the like. It got to where noh was only performed in Kyoto. This type of aversion was gradually reevaluated, but people in the early Meiji had just come out of a war, so the Tokugawa shogunate was a target for hatred.

Later, people came to see some good in the Edo period. For example, literary figures who had developed a penchant for France started noticing similarities between that country and Edo-period Japan. Late Meiji writers associated with the Pan Society[2], such as Kinoshita Mokutarō (1885–1945) and Kitahara Hakushū (1885–1942), likened shogunate corruption to the atmosphere in Europe at the end of the eighteenth century. Nagai Kafū (1879–1959) loved the Chinese-style poetry from

---

2. A society of poets and Western-style painters.

the late Edo period for that reason, and other people also began to longingly praise the Bunka (1804–1817) and Bunsei (1818–1830) periods. That trend among literary scholars continued for many years.

Of course, the most dramatic changes came after the Second World War. In two stages, in fact. The first was immediately after the war, from 1945 until around 1955, when the early modern period was considered the worst in Japan's history. Watsuji Tetsurō's *Closed Borders* is an example of that view. Writers frequently emphasized the antipathy ordinary people of the Edo period felt for those in power. When I first came to Japan in 1953, everyone called things they didn't like "feudalistic." Of course, feudalism is closely associated with the early modern era, so using that word as a pejorative shows what people thought about that period of Japan's past.

But then around 1962 or 1963 I started to see a different opinion arise. First, people started to think isolationism wasn't necessarily a bad thing. The idea was that if Europeans like Kaempfer who were actually here during that time thought the Edo period was great, it can't have been as bad as everyone was saying after the war. The next stage in that line of thought was that Japan had everything it needed in the Edo period, including a highly developed culture, so there was no need for contact with or imports from other countries. Well, maybe a few imports here and there, but not much.

Today it seems like Japan's early modern period is garnering even stronger support. At least, its critics are now in the minority. So over a relatively short period of time, there's been an about-face on the issue.

Shiba Things are definitely different now. I was born in the 1920s, like you, so I grew up thankful that I didn't have to live through Japan's feudal era. I'm sure there were plenty of wonderful things about it, though...

The most famous saying about Japan's feudal period is by author and educator Fukuzawa Yukichi (1835–1901), who said "Feudalism killed my father." Fukuzawa's father was a very, very serious man, a minor official at a rice storehouse in Osaka. He worked very hard for a salary of just 13 *koku*[3]—barely enough to keep his family fed—and died suddenly when he was 45 years old. He was very fond of study, and was highly regarded by scholars even beyond his domain of Buzen–Nakatsu [present-day Ōita prefecture], but for whatever reason he was unable to become more than an ordinary accountant. Fukuzawa would apparently break down in tears when recalling his father's hard life. Not that he ever knew his father, since he was only two years old when he died, and he probably had a somewhat idealized image based on stories he heard from his mother, but in any case, it seems he blamed feudalism for the pain and suffering that characterized his father's life.

As you mentioned, many noh actors lost their jobs during the Meiji Restoration, but so did many other domain-sponsored artists. Painters could feed themselves if they had a supply of screens and the like in need of decorating, but I can't imagine there was much demand. Losing their government salaries must have been quite a blow for most of them. So in many ways, the Meiji period really was a revolution.

But one of its biggest shortcomings was that the Meiji government was formed by people with low social standing and limited cultural knowledge. They mostly ignored the various threads of academic thought that had started to appear in the Edo period, instead drawing only from Neo-Confucianism. They started out as major proponents of the West, but around 1882 or 1883, they got this idea of creating a truly "Japanese" country, and started rewriting all the textbooks and what have you to better reflect Neo-Confucian values and ideologies.

As we can see from its five-hundred-year history in Korea, Neo-Confucianism is a very hollow theology. I'd even call it a false teaching. So it's a little disappointing that the teachings of Edo figures like Ogyū Sorai (1666–1728) and Itō Jinsai (1627–1705) were set aside in favor of a poor choice like Neo-Confucianism. So much was lost as a result. And it wasn't until around 1962 or 1963 that people suddenly started to realize that.

---

3. Koku: A unit of volume used to measure rice, originally about 280 liters.

Keene It's interesting that the Meiji period was a time when people who up to that point had mainly been peasants had the opportunity to create a new government, allowing more people to live the kinds of lives they wanted, and that a similar kind of thing happened after the Second World War. The end of the war meant that previously persecuted thinkers could now freely express their ideas, allowing them to harshly condemn Japan's past. But once that phase ended, the past was largely forgotten. People substituted idealized images of drinking sake while staring at the moon or the pretty Sumida river of yesteryear for the harsher realities of the actual past.

Images like that make modern-day Japanese forget how hard life was for commoners in early modern Japan. Even people who are aware of that reality tend to set it aside as uninteresting, and instead focus on what seems like fun.

Shiba That might also be a backlash from the overly harsh criticism of the early modern period that came in the Meiji period, and after the Second World War.

Keene Yes, the criticism was overly harsh. When I first arrived as a study-abroad student, books about Bashō would go out of their way to emphasize that he was a simple farmer, not a samurai, and describe how he was always resisting the Tōdō clan. It's almost like it would have been embarrassing otherwise—that it was somehow shameful to have been born into a samurai clan. Proving that the Chinese Song dynasty poet Su Shi wasn't a noble was another significant academic pursuit at the time.

Shiba What an interesting sign of the times. It seems that starting around the Muromachi period Bashō's family lived in the home of some local lord in Iga, and during the Edo period they became prosperous farmers. Well-off farmers had money, and by supporting a samurai clan or making donations, they could get a son promoted to be a samurai. A second son, at least—the eldest would stay home. The low-ranking samurai position of *chūgoshō* was perfect for such second sons, and could be purchased cheaply. I'm not sure what exactly chūgoshō did, but anyway Bashō became one.

I believe that Kayano Sanpei—who the character Kanpei in *Chūshingura* is based on—is from Settsu–Ibaraki [Osaka], near where Kawabata Yasunari (1899–1972) was born. Kawabata was born in a large home, but his Kayano home was even larger, and still exists today. Apparently, a small domain of just 50,000 koku called Akō was established in Banshū [modern-day western Hyōgo prefecture]. They needed samurai, and Sanpei became one through family connections. The Kayanos had been a samurai clan back in the Warring States era, but they were demoted to farmers in the Edo period. Even so, they could claim samurai heritage and were permitted to have at least one in the family, and I think Bashō became one in a similar manner. So if somebody called him "a simple farmer" to his face, I think he'd have gotten pretty mad. [Laughs]

Keene Of all his disciples, Bashō had a particular bond with Morikawa Kyoriku (1656–1715), who was a samurai through and through. I'm sure that recognizing him as a fellow samurai was part of their connection. But his status as a commoner or a noble doesn't change the value of what he wrote. The literature he produced is a world treasure, so even if he was a samurai, I don't think we can hold it against him. [Laughs]

Shiba [Laughs for some time]

Keene Anyway, periods in which it is fashionable to decry Japan's early modern period inevitably create a backlash, and sure enough we now see people claiming it wasn't all that bad. The more extreme proponents call it a very good time, or even the best of times.

Shiba If nothing else, people back then seem to have had better manners than we do now—at least people of a certain stature. By "a certain stature," I don't just mean samurai and nobility—any farming village would certainly have had five or six refined homes. That's what I'm talking about. They had very good manners, but a very impoverished daily life.

For instance, in Yoshida Shōin's (1830–1859) family home, in Hagi in the Chōshū domain [Yamaguchi prefecture], they only served fish once each month. This was a fairly well-to-do, 60-koku home, but Yoshida wrote that his father worshipped fish. Not that he literally worshipped fish, I imagine, but that he was deeply grateful to be able to eat fish once a month. That's how poor people were. Fukuzawa Yukichi's hometown of Nakatsu was so poor that pretty much only the castle had ceramic roofing tiles in his day. So no matter how much one wants to idealize the Edo period, it was a time of extreme poverty.

Keene Maybe so, but compared to Europe back then, I think the standard of living was higher in Japan. Foreigners residing in Japan, like Townsend Harris (1804–1878) in Shimoda, likely had various complaints, but their writings don't mention the Japanese being particularly poor, or starving. They say the Japanese were quite healthy, in fact. It's probably true that one could only get fish once a month, but it seems everyone was doing well enough on a plant-based diet. I'm sure it would seem like a terrible life as compared to the Japan of today, but people were probably better off here than in Europe.

Shiba You think so? I suppose it's hard to measure in detail, that it depends on what you compare... But maybe you're right. They didn't write about extreme poverty, at least.

There are some records written by the Dutch at Nagasaki in the late Edo period, when Willem Huyssen van Kattendijke (1816–1866) was in Japan as commandant of the Nagasaki Naval Training Center. In his journal, he wonders why Japanese farmers were so poor despite being in such an agriculturally bountiful country, and concludes that it can only be because the shogunate or the daimyos took too much from them. I guess that's about the extent of people writing about life in

Japan being poor.

Keene   An older Dutch friend of mine told me that in his grandfather's day—which I guess would have been the mid-nineteenth century—the farmers in Holland didn't really have summer clothing and winter clothing. They just wore the same thing year-round. It would get hot, of course, and their pants would get so stiff with sweat that they could stand on their own, but they would just wear the same clothes all year, no matter how dirty they got or how bad they smelled. The Japanese might have been poor, but at least they had summer clothing and winter clothing, and they bathed when they could. They were near naked while working in rice paddies, but they dressed up for special occasions. I can't help but think that the Dutch must have been jealous when they saw how clean the Japanese were.

Shiba   Possibly so. Speaking of van Kattendijke, one of his pupils was Katsu Kaishū (1823–1899). In his journal, van Kattendijke highly praises Katsu as, perhaps not a revolutionary, but as a very innovative thinker.

Katsu Kaishū was extremely dissatisfied with classism. He was a shogunate retainer, but a very low-ranking one. When he later sailed the *Kanrin-maru* to America and back, and met with the lords at Edo castle to tell them what kind of country America was, he told them something they didn't want to hear—that "America is a place where it's talent that takes you to the top." [Laughs] That's a report that strikes directly at the core problem with feudalism, and demonstrates Katsu's dissatisfaction very well. When he sailed the *Kanrin-maru* to America I'm sure he considered himself captain, but Kimura Kaishū (1830–1901), the son of a noble family, was assigned as commander. Kimura was a good man, but still, Katsu got into a sulk on the voyage and refused to leave his cabin. His depression peaked in the middle of the Pacific, and he demanded that a lifeboat be lowered so that he could return to Edo alone. That's how much he hated the class system.

Keene I suppose young people today who think the early modern era was a good time picture themselves as nobles, never as someone in the lower ranks of society. [Laughs]

Shiba Everyone imagines themselves in a starring role.

Keene And therein lies the rub. Life as a French noble was pretty good, up until the revolution. But not everyone gets to be born a noble. That's the problem.

The Edo Spirit of Play

Shiba There's been some interesting research on the French Revolution in the past decade or so. It paints a very different picture from what we learned in school.

Keene Yes, quite the opposite in fact.

Shiba Bashō's family was able to buy him status because they were very well off, although he didn't earn it himself. Just like Bashō, and like Kanpei in *Chūshingura*, wealthy French townsfolk—the bourgeoisie—could buy themselves position before the Revolution.

Keene And I'm sure they did.

Shiba In France, that was the highest they attained. So one theory is that the French Revolution was the result of resentment about that limitation.

Keene I imagine that author Higuchi Ichiyō (1872–1896) must have had a very difficult life. She owned a store, but it didn't bring in enough money to support her. Even so, she prided herself on being "a daughter of nobles." But while her father had bought himself position as a samurai, he was the first in her family who could make such a claim. She knew that, of course, but she still considered herself nobility.

Shiba   I suppose all cultures value perseverance in the face of poverty, but the samurai class in Japan's Edo period seems to be an extreme example of that.

Keene   That's right. "Pride even when hungry," as they used to say.

Shiba   Anyway, the samurai were not a wealthy lot. Every farming village had a home or three that was better off, not to mention merchants in the towns. The samurai were poor, but, well, they had their own aesthetic about it, and townsfolk like Ihara Saikaku loved them for it. Without that respect, the samurai would just be a bunch of paupers.

Keene   Saikaku's writing is always respectful of the samurai. He doesn't have a bad thing to say.

Shiba   To a fault, actually.

Keene   Sure. "We merchants do such-and-such a thing, but a samurai would never stoop so low," things like that.

Shiba   Lafcadio Hearn's (1850–1904) wife was the daughter of a samurai. She told him all this stuff about how a samurai lives and thinks, and apparently he believed that a samurai must always be true to his word. There was a story about how a samurai promised to be at a certain place at a certain time, and when he found himself unable to be there, he committed seppuku so that at least his spirit could go in place of his body. Not a true story, of course, but it shows how people idealized the samurai like Saikaku did, even in the days when samurai were right in front of them. And this idolization intensified from the Meiji on.

Johan Huizinga (1872–1945) praises Japan throughout his book

Homo Ludens. He says that bushido is play, just like chivalry was play, and I was happy just to see that he included samurai in that sentiment alongside knights. If it wasn't play—in Huizinga's sense of the term, mind you—then you couldn't have seppuku, and you couldn't stand tall in the face of poverty. The Edo period was rich with that spirit of play.

Keene   Japan's early modern era was indeed one of play. Haiku started out as a form of play, as did the kind of literature that Saikaku wrote, *ukiyo-zōshi.* Kabuki was play, and so was ukiyo-e. In a sense, red-light districts were the cultural centers of the early modern era. Many forms of literature were born there, and they also had a close connection with theater. I'm not sure what things are like now, but until around thirty years ago, if you had problems getting kabuki tickets you could get them from a geisha. There were all kinds of relationships like that.

Ukiyo-e were something like advertisements for prostitutes. After the all-women kabuki shows that were popular for a time, VIPs would visit the dressing rooms and spend the evening with the performers. Fights between theater-goers aiming for the same woman became so frequent that the shogunate closed down the theaters for a while. But there was always an element of play.

Shiba   The Soemonchō district in Osaka is quite a bustling place today, but when we were kids it was a charming area, all teahouses. And the Dōtonbori district is full of movie theaters now, but you can still get a sense of the theaters that used to be there.

There was this author from Osaka, Fujisawa Takeo, who died recently in his eighties. His mother lived into her nineties and talked about how when she was a girl in the 1880s, her favorite thing to do was to go to the theaters in Dōtonbori. They didn't have them in Tokyo, but in Osaka there were these theater teahouses. She would go to one and have a light meal, then change clothes before entering the theater. Then she'd return to the teahouse during intermission and change clothes again. She said she looked forward to it so much that she couldn't sleep the night before. That custom lasted until the late 1880s—it's a shame that it died out.

Keene When I was living in a dorm in Kyoto, an elderly woman told me a similar story about how excited she would get the night before going to the Minami-za kabuki theater in Shijō. She could only go out a few times a year, so going to the theater was a moment of great liberation. At the theater, she was free to watch what she wanted, and talk to friends—it was a very different atmosphere from today's National Theater. Going there is like being in a classroom—everyone is paying such close attention, even wearing earphones to listen to narratives. People had more fun back then. They didn't care if they missed the finer points of the play. Today it's more like studying. Watching kabuki is a very different experience.

Shiba Speaking of the world of play, [looks at tokonoma] the picture on this scroll was painted by Suga Tatehiko, who isn't well known in Tokyo, just in Osaka. Even in Osaka most people have forgotten him— he was seventy-something in 1955, so if he were alive today he would be around 110 or 120 years old. I often visited his home when doing research, and he would tell me about the old days. The Japanese government started an art show called the Japan Fine Arts Exhibition in 1907. In those days there were no art dealers—art was sold by scroll mounters. Suga was quite famous in Osaka in 1907, so a scroll mounter came to Suga one day, and told him about this art exhibition that the government was sponsoring. Suga was a true man of the Edo period, and said in his typically modest way, "I cannot believe that government elites would have any interest in a scribbler like myself." [Laughs] The seventy-something Suga that I knew was the same Edo townsman—simple, understated, and deferential. He was a really good man.

Keene Meeting someone like that makes me want to visit those days.

CHAPTER 3
Meiji Melancholy

Natsume Sōseki

Shiba   Japan at the end of the 270-year-long Edo period was like a mature adult. But as soon as the Meiji period began, Edo customs and everything else were cast aside in favor of new cultural systems—what people back then called "civilization and enlightenment." Culturally speaking, it's like Japan reverted to being a child again. I guess that requires some explanation. What I mean is that compared to Europe and the United States, Japan was the youngest actor on the world stage. Many Japanese had a hard time adjusting to that as they studied abroad in Europe and tried to adapt to Western learning, but I think Natsume Sōseki (1867–1916) and Mori Ōgai (1862–1922) are the best examples.

I have my own pet theory about the melancholy that these writers express, namely that when they returned to Japan from the West they didn't have anyone to talk to. Their wives hadn't had any kind of higher education, so they couldn't really talk with them about the ideas they had encountered in Europe, nor did their friends truly understand the damage their souls suffered by having one foot in Europe and one in Japan. As a result, we see this kind of melancholy that's peculiar to Meiji-period intellectuals…

I think Sōseki in particular was a sort of perfect Edo man before he studied in England. But over there, he was just some funny little guy from a foreign land, and looking at himself in the mirror probably sowed the seeds of an inferiority complex. Since his studies were supported by the Ministry of Education, he would have been expected to attend Cambridge or the like, but he couldn't bring himself to do so. He just couldn't see himself enjoying university life while rubbing shoulders with the children of the British elite.

You've spoken before about how well Sōseki wrote in English, but he actually learned it by talking with the landladies of the many boarding-houses where he stayed in South London. He probably learned some Cockney dialect from them that wouldn't have been understood any-where else. Rather than attend university as was expected of him, he found an Irish tutor, William James Craig (1843–1906), and spent all of his time studying in Craig's attic. It seems odd that he would go all the way to London to study Shakespeare in an Irish professor's attic. One would think that he would at least have attended classes at University College, London [where he was enrolled], but he apparently didn't think he deserved that much.

While Sōseki was in England, he met Ikeda Kikunae (1864–1936), who later went on to discover monosodium glutamate. People in the sciences found it easier to stand as equals to Westerners. They could go to a research institute or whatever in Germany to study chemistry, like Ikeda did, and return to Japan after they'd learned some new tech-nique, so there was no need to feel inferior. From what I understand, speaking with Ikeda was very comforting for Sōseki. Not only was Sōseki a literature student, he was in England on orders from the Japanese government to study English language instruction or some-thing like that—in other words, to train himself how to teach English, which was misery for him. Ikeda could get by without much language ability, as long as he understood the chemical symbols.

I don't know much about what happened when Sōseki returned to Japan, but apparently he followed the Ministry of Education's plan for him—to teach at the Tokyo Imperial University and to eventually take over Lafcadio Hearn's position as lecturer there.

But that equated to stealing Hearn's position. Sōseki didn't write about it, but Hearn likely wasn't thrilled by that situation, especially considering that when he became a Japanese citizen he took a drastic hit to his paycheck, which went from the exorbitant salary paid to foreign government advisors to the standard rate for Japanese instructors. And now this Natsume fellow comes along. But as it turns out, Sōseki was damaged by his time in England, and wanted to avoid becoming an English teacher if at all possible. It seems he just wanted to go back to being his old man-of-Edo self.

If you read Sōseki's *Bungaku-ron* [Theory of Literature] or *Bungaku hyōron* [Literary Criticism], he talks about how it's the prose and poetry of China that he considers real literature, while the literature of Europe and Britain is a very different kind of thing. He expresses a kind of longing for Chinese literature and poetry. Somewhere he wrote about how much he wished he'd been sent to study abroad in Beijing, rather than England. Of course, the Ministry of Education would never do that since it had already pegged him as an English teacher, but it shows how much he wanted to escape from all that.

In the end Sōseki left the Imperial University and accepted an offer from the *Asahi shimbun* newspaper. When Ph.D. degrees in literature were later established, he refused to accept one, despite being asked to, and despite the fact that receiving a Ph.D. in literature at the time was even more prestigious than receiving the Order of Culture award. Kōda Rohan (1867–1947) accepted a Ph.D. degree, but Sōseki refused. Sōseki wrote somewhere that he wasn't at all that thrilled to become a member of a French academy. I don't think having a Japanese Ph.D. in literature is quite the same as being a member of a French literary academy, but anyway it shows that he just wanted to be an ordinary man—just Natsume Sōseki. He wanted to escape from this Meiji-esque "civilization and enlightenment," which he found so difficult to cope with.

Sōseki was in very poor emotional health during his stay in London— what people at the time would have called "neurotic"—because he felt like the entire weight of European culture was on his shoulders. The only people who didn't seem to feel that way were technical students like Ikeda Kikunae. Around the same time, Sōseki's high-school classmate Akiyama Saneyuki (1868–1918), an Imperial Navy officer, was studying in the United States. He wasn't a typical study-abroad student, but instead a military attaché studying naval strategy under Captain Alfred Mahan (1840–1914). Mahan was quite an exceptional person. Before him naval battles were seen as just a bunch of warships slugging it out, but he introduced tactics and strategies into the equation, turning naval warfare into an academic pursuit. Learning that stuff is similar to researching technology, so Akiyama was able to return to Japan without feelings of inadequacy.

But studying language and literature like Sōseki did, that was a lot of pressure, so much so that when he returned to Japan, he just wanted to get away from the entire world of English. Stories like that make me think it must have been hard to be an intellectual in the Meiji period. What do you think?

Keene   I think that most people born in the early modern era—those who were alive in the Meiji period but had received an Edo education and still engaged in Edo ways of thinking—reacted to European culture in one of three ways.

The first group rejected it. They considered themselves strictly Japanese, and therefore had no need for foreign things.

The second group resisted European ideas, but still used them. Natsume Sōseki is a perfect example, in that his novels were based on a European model, which was nothing like the frivolous *gesaku* works of the Edo period. Even so, he resisted to the very end.

The third group wholeheartedly embraced foreign influences. Natural scientists like Ikeda, who you mentioned, are good examples, as is Mori Ōgai in most respects. He was strongly influenced by studying in Germany, and he never showed any resistance to those influences. He never criticized Germany, and he never said that the Japanese should reject foreign ideas.

People who received an Edo education and rejected new forms of culture looked foolish. That was true in novels as well as real life. Take Ōnuma Chinzan (1818–1891). He wrote excellent Chinese-style poetry even into the Meiji period. He hated the name "Tokyo" and continued to call the capital "Edo." He kept his hair in a topknot until he died in

1891, which at the time must have made him seem quite silly. He was always rejecting the modern age in his writing, always going on about what a wonderful time the Bunka (1804–1818) and Bunsei (1818–1830) periods were, how back then everyone had the time to drink sake and watch the moon at Yanagibashi, how that's the right way to live, and how the modern age didn't suit the Japanese, or any human being for that matter.

A slightly different example is the protagonist Bunzō in Futabatei Shimei's (1864–1909) *Ukigumo* [The Drifting Cloud]. He doesn't directly reject Western influences, but he still adheres to Confucianism. His friend Noboru, in contrast, is a man of the new age. He cajoles his boss to gain favor, which results in his being promoted. Bunzō can't do that, he's too set in his ways. His Confucian beliefs tell him that flattery is abhorrent, but this leads him to failure. He's so weak and powerless that it's hard not to sympathize with him a little, but in the end he just looks foolish.

The worst off were those in the second group—those who accepted European and foreign things, but only grudgingly, and were miserable because of it. Sōseki's protagonist in *Sorekara* [And Then] is an example. He talks repeatedly in that novel about the horrible fate of the Japanese, who have to go forth into this world that Westerners made, and how hard that will be. Sōseki wholly rejects European literature in *Kusamakura* [Grass Pillow], saying that the pure world of Chinese poetry can't be found in European literature, where everything is tainted with the stench of business and money. He also complains that the superhuman world depicted in Du Fu's (712–770) poetry can't be found in European poetry. But all this is happening in a book that isn't at all in the traditional Japanese form. Its structure is highly influenced by Europe… You can't write a haiku-style novel, no matter how hard you try. Novels just aren't that short. That caused Sōseki a lot of anxiety. His *Wagahai wa neko de aru* [I am a Cat] has some Edo-like elements, but that's the last book of his that does.

Sōseki never stops showing this resistance to Western culture, but Mori Ōgai doesn't show it at all, despite having received a similar education. He appraises the West more fairly. I think Sōseki was already thirty years old when he went to Europe, but Ōgai was younger. That made him more flexible. He was able to remain calm and offer counter-arguments when someone said something disparaging about Japan. When I read Ōgai's journals and novels from that time, I'm really struck by what a wonderful person he was. He doesn't reject his identity as a Japanese, he embraces it. Even so, he realizes that the Japanese in this new Japan of the Meiji period have to learn the natural sciences and mathematics and such. As an interesting aside, I read that once when he was on a train, Ōgai met a German man who wanted a photograph of him. The man was an anthropologist, so I guess he found Ōgai's face to be curious. Anyway, Ōgai agreed to give him the photo, but on one condition—that he give Ōgai a photo of himself in return. I think that's just the perfect answer.

Shiba   I agree. Just giving the man a photograph would be like providing him with an anthropological specimen. His condition made for a clever repartee.

Keene   Anyway, once the Meiji period began, it became nearly impossible to stick to old-style morality. People in the Meiji period wanted to be important and improve their position. But Confucianism doesn't allow that. A Confucian merchant can't study to become a man of virtue. The concept just isn't there.

The idea that waking up early and working hard is all it takes to get ahead is a very Western one. But people thought that way in Meiji Japan, which in turn meant that people who didn't share those ideals and instead stuck to the old morality had no real place—people like Bunzō in *The Drifting Cloud*, who was so stubbornly honest that he couldn't flatter someone he didn't hold in high regard. It was a new society, one that had no need for people like Bunzo.

Of course, I think that Japanese who grew up under the influence of the early modern era reacted in various ways to the Meiji era. Those reactions depended on individual personalities, and on the circumstances of each life, so it's impossible to make generalizations that apply universally.

The Spirit of Independence among Commoners

Shiba   Indeed, not everyone is the same. My grandfather, Fukuda Sōhachi, was a farmer, but he came to Osaka from a suburb of Banshū–Himeji called Hiro [Hirohata] in the first year of the Meiji period. He was just a boy then, but he says he wore his hair in a topknot until 1905, the year the Russo-Japanese War ended. He claimed to have been the last man in Japan to do so. [Laughs]

My grandfather was a true exclusionist. He didn't suffer from a lack of money, but he considered elementary school to be a Western thing. He acquiesced and sent his two daughters to school, but when he had a boy at age fifty—that would be my father—he couldn't send his precious son to such a place. This made things hard for my father. He had to undergo a draft inspection when he was twenty years old, and at that time he was supposed to present an elementary school diploma. Of course, having never attended elementary school he didn't have one, so apparently he bribed a school principal in Osaka to produce one. Then came the certification exam. By then my grandfather wasn't around, and my father had been raised by his sister, who was twenty years older than him. As was frequently done in Osaka in those days, his sister supported them by taking in adopted children.

Anyway, instead of sending the son he had at the age of fifty to elementary school, my grandfather sent him to a private school supposedly associated with the Matsudaira clan, which taught the Chinese classics. I guess back then there were still people around who taught subjects like that. What's interesting, though, is that my father was also sent to a private English language school, and to a private school that taught algebra. From what I understand you can do at least elementary algebra using an abacus, hard as that is to imagine. My grandfather was from the suburbs of Himeji, so he learned *wasan*, the Edo-period Japanese mathematics of Seki Takakazu (1642–1708). Anyway, my grandfather was an anachronism of a kind you don't really see any more.

To give an example of how different things were back then, I heard that when my father came home from math school, my grandfather would use wasan to check the answers to his algebra problems. I'm not sure how you accommodate the x's and y's of algebra when doing that, but that's what I was told.

In any case, in my grandfather's day there were still commoners who stuck to the old Edo ways, but after Japan won in the Russo-Japanese war, men gave up their topknots and adopted a more Western hairstyle. They also started buying pocket watches and Western-style umbrellas. There was a sense that winning the war made it okay to adopt such Western items, not just among the intelligentsia, but commoners as well.

As you said, during the middle of the Edo period this idea emerged that if you just work or study harder you can make something of yourself. At the end of the Edo period, the Tokugawa shogunate sent Nakamura Masanao (1832–1891) to study in England, but he had to return just a year or two later when the shogunate collapsed. He brought a book with him on the return voyage, which happened to be *Self-Help* by Samuel Smiles (1812–1904). Nakamura was a Tokugawa vassal, so he was to be relocated to Shizuoka along with the rest. He translated *Self-Help* on the boat, hoping to make the other vassals read it during their exile and thereby convince them to find some way to stand on their own feet. It ended up being a bestseller through the end of the Meiji period, alongside Fukuzawa Yukichi's *Seiyō jijō* [Things Western].

Smiles was a doctor and editor of a local newspaper, and he wrote *Self-Help* as a kind of folk philosophy. But Nakamura translated it for the betterment of Japan, on par with the *Analects of Confucius* or the *Mencius*. And he intended it not for the general public, but for his peers, the former vassals of the Tokugawa shogunate. That's how the Meiji period started. Already, in the Edo period, people like Ninomiya Sontoku (1787–1856) and Ishida Baigan (1685–1744) had been pushing Shingaku, a Japanese brand of Neo-Confucianism that said people could get ahead through hard work, despite Chinese insistence that the small were destined to remain small. Shingaku agreed perfectly with the Protestant work ethic of the English, that spirit of self-reliance through hard work.

Keene That's right. There's a monument to Nakamura Masanao in Izu, at Usami. It says, "Heaven helps those who help themselves." I knew I had heard that saying somewhere else, and when I looked into it I found that it was a Benjamin Franklin quote. So sure, those ideas were around in Edo-period Japan, particularly the mid-Edo. If you read Saikaku's stories about Edo townsfolk, they're always waking up early and working hard, without wasting time. They say things like "If you fall down, pick up a rock while getting back up." And he blesses his hard workers with a very Franklinesque prosperity in the end.

Of course, I think that the groundwork laid out by people like Saikaku and Ishida was requisite to Japan's change—without it, the Japanese probably wouldn't have been able to adopt Western ideas as easily as they did in the Meiji period. It was that background that enabled them to accept Western thinking without rebelling against it. It must have been much harder for the Chinese—they didn't have an equivalent to the culture of Edo townsfolk.

Shiba Not in China, no.

Keene But in Japan, setting Saikaku aside, Ishida Baigan's version of Shingaku in particular said that even merchants could lead a splendid life. He insisted that such things weren't the sole province of the samurai, and I consider that to be quite a conclusion.

Shiba It is indeed. As an interesting comparison with China, fifteen or sixteen years ago in Beijing there was an exhibition of work by Higashiyama Kaii (1908–1999). His paintings are very large and heavy—they must weigh around four hundred kilograms each—so you can't hold them up using small nails. The exhibition was sponsored by the *Nihon Keizai shimbun* newspaper and the Japan–China Cultural

Exchange Association, the director of which was Shirato Norio. He showed up at the exhibition space beforehand to make sure the nails were strong enough, and if any of them looked weak he would ask that they be reinforced. While he was doing this some Chinese official showed up and said something like "Mr. Shirato, you shouldn't be doing this kind of thing." In other words—my own words, mind you—menial tasks like that, actually moving about and doing things, were for less important people. The official thought that as one of the event's primary organizers, Shirato should sit back and let other people do the work.

That's a big difference between Japan and China. Both countries were primarily Confucian, but Edo Japan had this Protestant-like idea that you mentioned—that hard work was the path to success. I think that's what made the Meiji period possible.

I've gotten a little sidetracked here, but let me share one more story that I love.

Sir Harry Smith Parkes (1828–1885), British consul general in the late Edo period, started out as a non-career official at the embassy in Canton. He was young and learned Chinese very quickly. That led to rapid promotions, first to interpreter, then to secretary, and eventually to Consul General in Japan. So anyway, when Parkes was still a young man, the governor of the Qing dynasty came to speak with him at the British Consulate. He arrived in a procession with musicians and all that. So many Chinese came that there weren't enough chairs, and the consulate had to scramble to find some. Supposedly, the consul himself rolled up his sleeves and was arranging chairs when the governor encountered him. The governor said, "Who is this? I cannot speak with such a low-ranking person," and left. [Laughs] I think this type of attitude has greatly delayed China's modernization.

Confucianism and Empiricism

Keene Confucianism was at the heart of early-modern Japanese thought. There were many outstanding Confucianists during that era, but very few by the end of the Edo period (1600–1868). The thread of Confucian thought also became narrower and more meager, so that in the end it was all about loyalty.

I think that actually ended up benefiting present-day Japan, but the Confucianism of the late Tokugawa shogunate was far from first-rate philosophy. In the middle of the Tokugawa reign, some unique people like Ogyū Sorai (1666–1728) and Itō Jinsai (1627–1705) had opposed what later developed into Neo-Confucianism. They instead promoted Kogaku [Ancient Learning], which traced its roots back to the foundations of Confucianism. That didn't last for long, however. In the end, Edo Confucianism became what I suppose you could call a system of manners, which I think is one reason there's so little crime in Tokyo. Many of the economically advanced Asian countries have probably been influenced by Confucianism, but as a philosophy it's pretty much dead. I can't think of any real advancement in Confucian thought since the middle of the Edo period.

Shiba   Now that you mention it, I can't either. In China there was Kaozheng, which was similar to what Ogyū Sorai taught, but—and maybe I'm being biased here—I think that just as Sorai was a little ahead of his time, Kaozheng came about fifty years too soon. As an example from the mid-Edo, Arai Hakuseki (1657–1725) came from a Neo-Confucian background, but he wasn't very Neo-Confucian. He was an empiricist who believed what his eyes told him. I think this was because Neo-Confucianism had less of an influence in Japan than it did in Korea and China, where it permeated everything, and because the Japanese learned Neo-Confucianism half on their own, which resulted in it becoming a unique ideology.

There was one other faction—one that I don't know all that much about—that was based in the Nanbu domain in northeastern Japan, what's now Morioka in Iwate prefecture and part of Akita prefecture. This faction was sort of a post-Meiji compromise between Neo-Confucianism and Ogyū Sorai. I'm not sure exactly what the compromise consisted of, but it produced some interesting thinkers like Naitō Konan (1866–1934) and Kanō Kōkichi (1865–1942), who insisted that one should examine the world directly with one's own eyes, rather than through the filter of Neo-Confucian ideology. When you include thinkers like that, there was quite a lot of variety in Japanese Confucianism. But as you said, it was running out of steam by the end of the Edo period.

Speaking of manners, in a book I wrote about Sakamoto Ryōma (1836–1867) around thirty years ago, I described Ryōma as an uneducated man. There was another man named Hirai, a friend of Ryōma's from a similar background, who had a very attractive younger sister. Ryōma sent her a love letter, and this being the end of the Edo period, when propriety was all-important, she showed it to her brother. He said something like, "Watch out for Ryōma, he's an uneducated man."

A fan of Ryōma's once protested that assessment to me, saying "He can write, and he composed this lovely letter, so of course he's educated." But being "educated" at that time meant moral training and knowledge of Neo-Confucianism. So what her brother meant was that Ryōma was a man without rules. Who knew what he might do! There weren't many people like Ryōma in the late Edo period, when Confucianism was all about rules. Those rules provided safety, at least when everyone followed them...

Chūkō Shinsho published an interesting book called *Ondoru yawa* [Ondol Tales]. It was written by Yoon Hak-chun, a man slightly younger than me who was born into a *yangban* [Korean noble] family. He writes that a distant elderly relative once got angry at him for reciting Su Shi's poem *Chibi fu* [Ode on the Red Cliffs]. "Stop reading such unmanly things," he said. "You should be reading Confucius and Mencius." In other words, Neo-Confucianism was much stricter in Korea.

Keene   It was indeed. People weren't allowed to speak during meals, for example.

Shiba I heard that in Korea, up until the nineteenth century, you had to remove your eyeglasses in front of anyone older than you, because wearing eyeglasses could be interpreted as trying to look older than you really were. That would be unseemly, so removing your glasses was a form of courtesy.

Keene Well that's quite extreme, isn't it. In contrast, some Confucian scholars in the mid-Edo period wouldn't believe anything unless they saw it with their own eyes. Kaibara Ekken (1630–1714) is a good example. After hearing that there were only high waves and no low waves in Wakanoura, he went to see for himself. Upon arriving he said, "It was all a lie—there are all kinds of waves here, just like any other shore." [Laughs]

Shiba That sounds just like Kaibara Ekken. He was quite an individual.

Keene There's no poetic side to him—he's all prose. That's what makes him interesting.

Shiba Indeed. He lived just before the mid-Edo period, so I guess that about marks the end of scholarly inquiry into Confucianism. But "uneducated" folk like Sakamoto Ryōma and Hokkaido explorer Matsuura Takeshirō (1818–1888) wanted to see things for themselves.

Keene Matsuura Takeshirō was quite a man, as was Mogami Tokunai (1754?–1836), who came a little before him.

Shiba Their greatness stems from their lack of education. Lack of a solely Confucian education, that is—they studied things like astronomy and land surveying and map-making and mathematics.

Keene Right. There's a portrait of Mogami by Kawahara Keiga (1786–?) that really shows the man through his expression, unlike most portraits from that time. It's quite impressive.

Shiba   It shows the acuity and tenacity that allowed him to lead such a committed life, doesn't it.

Keene   In the eighteenth century, the Japanese came to highly value utility, particularly usefulness to one's country. In contrast to the Confucians, who tended to view all phenomena in terms of absolute "goodness" or "badness," scholars of Western learning asked whether those phenomena benefited the state, and supported whatever did. I think that idea might be related to Ishida Baigan.

For example, Honda Toshiaki (1743–1821) once looked at a foreign painting and said that it was a useful thing, unlike Japanese paintings, which were only pretty. When Japanese and Chinese paint a landscape, they try to capture its essence. That's not the approach Europeans took. To them, a painting had to serve a purpose. Honda was clearly thinking of book illustrations like the ones in European encyclopedias. Just by looking at them you could learn a lot, like how to make copperplates for instance. Japanese books didn't have anything like that. When the Japanese painted a picture, they wanted people to think it was beautiful, or something along those lines. You see that kind of thinking in all aspects of Japanese academics from back then.

Honda Toshiaki was impressed by how just 26 characters were enough to write any word in Dutch, while Japanese required tens of thousands of characters, plus two syllabaries. He actually wanted the Japanese to start writing in the Roman alphabet. In China, I don't think there's a sense even today that children spend too much time learning characters and therefore can't adequately study other subjects. I doubt any Chinese ever argued that characters should be given up in favor of the Roman alphabet. It probably would be harder to do with Chinese anyway, but in Japan I think that type of practical thinking was quite persistent.

Shiba   Most people in the Edo period thought that anything beneficial to society should be promoted. That spirit, or movement, grew even stronger as Western studies came to be permitted. Scholars of Western learning became more European in their thinking. For example, if a new treatment for a disease came out in a Dutch book, they would use their own money to publish that information in Japanese so people knew about it, without really worrying about making a profit. By contrast, the great practitioners of Chinese medicine—like Hanaoka Seishū (1760–1835), who researched anesthesia—tended to keep their findings secret and share them only with their successors. Students were even forbidden from spending time with students at other schools, to prevent secrets from leaking out. But when Dutch medicine arrived, things like, say, a new cholera treatment would be shared very quickly and widely.

I'm not sure which approach is more "Japanese." Regardless, when the era of Dutch studies started, Honda Toshiaki's way of thinking became immediately widespread, and Hanaoka Seishū's—the jealous guarding of secrets and passing down of knowledge only to apprentices—started to wane. For whatever reason, the Dutch way of doing things resonated with the Japanese, maybe because they really had always wanted to be more open…

The Nagasaki hospital built by Dutch doctor Pompe van Meerdervoort put all patients in the same room, regardless of their social standing. This caused a lot of consternation at first, but gradually, the idea that everyone is equal when they're sick took hold. People like Edo-era townsfolk and the wives of samurai had probably been thinking for a long time that all humans were equal, but once admitted to Pompe's hospital, they truly were. That's one way in which European culture started to work its way into Japan. Of course, many restrictions remained, even in the Meiji era.

Literacy Rates and "Ceremony"

Keene There's a similar sense of passing on secrets in today's art world. *Kyōgen* comic theater is one example, where *Tanuki no hara tsu-zumi* [The Tanuki's Belly Drum] is passed down from father to son. If the actor has three sons, he teaches it to the most talented one, and not the others. This kind of oral transmission of secrets has been practiced in Japan since long ago.

Scholars of Western learning were very surprised when they first saw a European encyclopedia, because everything was just written out, right there. Japanese researchers were used to selling their findings little by little. It's still like that in the world of noh drama. There are some noh songs that anyone can learn, but a slightly better song will cost you some money, and a very good one, one like *Sekidera komachi*, will cost you a small fortune. But Europeans were just writing everything down in books, so Japanese scholars wondered how they made a living.

In the early Edo period Hayashi Razan (1583–1657) gave public lectures on Confucianism, and Matsunaga Teitoku (1571–1653) lectured on poetry and essays, but that was considered to be quite unusual. Matsunaga Teitoku in particular got in big trouble with his teacher for the "sin" of giving away knowledge that had been personally imparted to him. From then on, though, it became ever more important to pass on knowledge to a wide variety of people.

The Japanese had printing technology since at least the Nara period (710–784), which they used occasionally to print sutras and things. They never printed literature, though, so there were no printed versions of the *Kojiki* [Records of Ancient Matters], or *Nihon shoki* [Chronicles of Japan], or the *Kokin wakashū* [Poems of Ancient and Modern Times] until the early modern period. Once printing machines started producing books in large quantities, however, everyone could read them. There was no need to get special permission or borrow the books from some great teacher. You could just buy them with your own money. This wasn't just a boon for education—it greatly changed society as a whole. I think it's quite significant that the masses were now able to read classic works, not just the nobility. More people were probably reading books in early modern Japan than in any European country. Europe only had those 26 characters, but that didn't do much to advance education there. Japan probably had the largest population of readers in the world.

Shiba   That might be related to the fact that unlike China and Korea, Japan never really had a system of civil service examinations. Those types of test seem to attract all the real talent, and anyone who doesn't feel they can pass doesn't bother to read books. Japan had no such system, but in Saikaku's time you couldn't become a clerk if you were illiterate, because you wouldn't be able to do the books or balance accounts. You might become a sailor, but never a captain. Everyone learned to read and write for practical purposes—to become a clerk or a captain or whatever—not so they could read high-brow works by great scholars.

But since everyone could read, they also had access to the writings of Saikaku, and they could write the occasional haiku. So that kind of thing spread to the masses.

Yosa Buson (1716–1784) wasn't fond of talking about his early life, but I think he was somehow related to a well-to-do farmer in the Osaka countryside. His haiku and other writings sometimes come across as a bit pedantic, showing off the extent to which he read Chinese classics. But you wouldn't have expected a figure like Buson to have emerged from the social class that he did in China or Korea.

In those countries, some people who failed the civil service exams went on to become scholars or write plays or novels. But, at the risk of repeating myself, I think that people in Japan had to learn to read and write and use an abacus just to captain a boat or whatever.

Keene   I didn't realize that literacy and numeracy were requirements for becoming a boat captain. Actually, I think that solves a mystery that I've been wondering about for some time now, about the first Japanese book translated by a non-Japanese—*Sangoku tsūran zusetsu* [An Illustrated Description of Three Countries], written by Hayashi Shihei (1738–1793) and published in Europe in 1832. It made its way to Europe via Siberia, which I had always found quite odd, because I had assumed that not only sailors but even their captains would have been illiterate. The three countries the book describes are Korea, Ryūkyū

[Okinawa], and Ezo [Hokkaido], so I'd bet that it originally belonged to a boat captain. Probably some European found it in the possession of a boat captain at a Japanese school in Siberia, and was able to translate it by asking him questions about it. Because the captain was literate! Quite interesting.

Shiba   There was a castaway named Dembei who became a teacher at a Japanese school by command of Peter the Great. Dembei was from a small Osaka town called Tanimachi, a town of wholesale businesses. Up until a little while ago, it was known for wholesale supply of copper materials. You know how sumo patrons are called *tanimachi*? Apparently that comes from a resident of Tanimachi who loved sumo and would often treat sumo wrestlers to meals. Anyway, Dembei was a young man whose father owned a pawnshop there, and he was sailing from Osaka to Edo when his ship met with a big storm. He ended up as a castaway in Russia, where he founded a Japanese school. Apparently he was considered something of a scholar in Russia, but in reality he was just this young heir to a pawnshop, not even from the port town of Osaka, but from one of its suburbs.

Normally, you wouldn't expect someone like that to be literate, but in Edo Japan he was literate by necessity. I think that Osaka probably had the highest literacy rate in Edo Japan, because it was a town of merchants and the home port for many sailors, due to the trade ships that were based there. That meant there were many schools teaching reading, writing, and arithmetic, and lots of private elementary schools, each with its own textbooks. Osaka was also a publishing town, and I've read somewhere that there were over ten thousand *ōraimono* primers in publication there at one point. I don't think that was because Osaka was a highly cultured city, but rather because there was demand for them.

Keene   That's probably true. Those primers all served a practical purpose. They don't really address proper ways of living or anything like that. They're all filled with things like the names of towns and addresses. [Laughs]

Shiba   Approaching the mid-Edo period, when Arai Hakuseki was still alive, a Korean diplomat named Sin Yu-han wrote a book called *Kaiyūroku* [Records of a Sea Voyage]. It's a remarkable travelogue, but the author clearly views the Japanese as being not quite human, almost bestial. Not surprising, I suppose, considering how leniently Confucianism was implemented in Japan, as compared to Korea. The book doesn't use the normal character for "person" when writing about the Japanese, but rather this other character, "*wa*." So a gathering of Japanese isn't a group of "people," but a group of "wa," which I guess is some other kind of human. He writes frequently about how bad Japanese writing and poetry in the Chinese style is. He meets with a hereditary daimyo, and with a lord of Tsushima, and writes about how stupid they all are. He also passes through Osaka, but writes nothing about how life there is dominated by a commodity-based economy. That's work for beasts, after all, not the path of a wise man.

While Sin Yu-han was on his way to Edo, people would approach him, asking him to write something, anything really. They were so thrilled to have a visitor from a land of wise sages. Sin Yu-han clearly agreed with them. The difference between the two countries is quite remarkable.

Keene   The Confucianism of China and Korea placed a heavy emphasis on ceremony and music. The Japanese didn't think about ceremony much, and so far as music goes, noh drama was about all they were interested in. Reading Chinese texts, it seems that ceremony was of central concern, but the Japanese just weren't all that interested. Music was totally out of the picture.

Shiba   Absolutely. We were talking about Harry Smith Parkes earlier. When Chinese governors visited the consulate where he worked, they would arrive with a procession blowing *suona* horns, so there's your music. And you can see the ritual aspect in the governor that refused to engage with someone who was acting like a subordinate—a meeting as equals with such a person would have been below his dignity. A lot of the ceremony derived from the rank of the person that one dealt with.

Sin Yu-han wasn't an envoy himself, just a record keeper. He had passed the civil service examinations, but he hadn't risen very high for someone who had passed the exams. The reason for that is clear: illegitimate children were looked down upon in Joseon, and that prevented him from getting ahead. I'm sure that was a depressing fact for him, but he was still part of a diplomatic corps dispatched by the King of Joseon, so he felt entitled to look down on some lord from Tsushima. The samurai of Tsushima considered their lord to be the greatest man in their domain, so they wanted to arrange a meeting with Sin Yu-han, but they met with a great deal of resistance. To a Korean envoy, the lord of Tsushima was just another vassal. Not that they used that word—I believe they called him something like a prince. But to them he was just some vassal to the shogun, which meant he was of a lower position. So by the measure of similarity of social rank, a meeting would not meet Confucian precepts of "ceremony."

I think contemporary Japanese are likely to confuse this concept of "ceremony" with the idea of being well-behaved, which today we would call "courtesy" or "manners." The Muromachi shogunate (1336–1573) developed this thing called the "Ogasawara-ryū School of Etiquette," which is the foundation for the modern Japanese sense of etiquette. But the Confucian idea of "ceremony" is a little bit different from etiquette in this sense, in a way that's hard for a modern person to understand. Actually, we're only talking about this because you brought it up—I don't think this is something that would come up between two Japanese. If we were to say "that guy has no manners," then we would be talking about etiquette. But "ceremony" in Confucianism is a much larger system, and it's harder to comprehend. So perhaps it's no surprise that Sin Yu-han found the Japanese to be beast-like.

Keene Koreans visiting China at the time even reported that the

Chinese had a less developed sense of ceremony than they did.

Shiba   The Koreans felt they were greatly superior to the Chinese. The Qing dynasty was created by the Jurchen, who they considered to be a much more barbaric people than themselves. This is all according to some complex calculation that I don't really understand. When Tokugawa Ienobu was shogun, back before Sin Yu-han arrived in Japan as a member of the envoy team, Arai Hakuseki received a Korean diplomatic mission in a very reserved manner, instead of the luxurious, solemn reception that the Koreans had expected. Considering the high value that the Koreans placed on ceremony, I guess it's no surprise that Arai's practical-mindedness caused them to consider him an "unceremonious *wa*."

CHAPTER 4
An Era for the Masses

What's Missing from Ukiyo-e

Keene   The art of the early modern period is wonderful. I just love it. Ukiyo-e and other art in that lineage is particularly beautiful. But aside from whether I love it or hate it, it had a huge impact on the West. I once went to a Paris art museum where famous artists each had their own section, and in the middle of each was a display of items from that artist's studio. Every one of them had ukiyo-e. Vincent van Gogh was clearly mimicking ukiyo-e.

Shiba   To van Gogh, Japan was all about ukiyo-e, and he blew that single aspect up into his own unique image.

Keene   Some artists intentionally copied them, completely digesting them and absorbing their influences. So I'm happy to admit the importance of ukiyo-e. But they always have an element of play to them. You never see elements of tragedy in ukiyo-e.

Shiba   Ah, interesting.

Keene   They are beautiful, yes, but they don't at all show the tragic aspects of life—human distress, things like that—that you see in European art from the same time or even earlier. It's just beauty. But it was a beauty unlike any in Europe, so Europeans did everything they could to absorb it.

But European art was darker, with deeper meaning. There was Japanese art like that in the Muromachi period and earlier, but those aspects don't rise to the surface in early-modern artworks. There are many early-modern images of the Buddha, but when I saw an exhibit in Tokyo of Buddha statues from the Guimet Museum in Paris, they weren't exactly the kind of thing that inspired faith. All that gold leaf…

Shiba   It's too beautiful.

Keene   Exactly. They aren't the kind of things that reflect an understanding of human suffering. They're very unlike Japanese Buddha images from before the Edo period. Those have a certain depth and solidity that you don't see much of in early-modern art. Not that I'm condemning the period for that. As I've said several times, I love that art. But it does lack solidity.

I even feel that way about the writings of Chikamatsu Monzaemon (1653–1725), the dramatist who I've studied the most. The Osaka that Chikamatsu describes is very impressive—it features in some of my favorite literature. But the characters are like dolls. They don't feel human, they don't demonstrate human depth. In *Sonezaki shinjū* [The Love Suicides at Sonezaki], when Tokubē is robbed by Kuheiji, whom he had considered a friend, his mind immediately turns to death, and nothing else. Watching the play, we have no idea why Tokubē would trust Kuheiji. I mean, we have no doubt that this is a bad guy, from the moment we see him. [Laughs] You can't help but think, why can't Tokubē *see* it? The *jōruri* puppets used in the show are very beautiful, so maybe that distracts you from such doubts…

Before jōruri, there was noh drama. Noh depicts a completely different world, one that represents the deepest aspects of humanity. European drama had similar elements, so I'm thankful that Japanese drama by people like Chikamatsu provided us with something different to think about. Viewed in light of theater throughout world history, however, Japanese drama feels like it's missing something.

Shiba   It does. Not to get too textbookish about it, but ukiyo-e inspired impressionist painters because they had learned that you had to look at things in terms of light and shadows, and use color to represent that, but ukiyo-e showed them that a single line could become a kimono, and that a face could be depicted just by its outline. It showed them a completely different way of doing things.

The paintings of Matisse were negatively influenced by ukiyo-e. They're completely flat. There were other European artists who had an interest in ukiyo-e but were able to retain the dimensionality of the European tradition. That was true of van Gogh at first, but as time passed, his "ukiyo-e disease" progressed. I'm not sure whether that was because ukiyo-e themselves are so wonderful or if it was due to some psychopathological reason. In the end, van Gogh said he wanted to go to Japan, but it may have just been because of how he symbolized Japan in his mind.

As you know, ukiyo-e artists used techniques similar to what photographers do now, like when Hiroshige (1797–1858) would place a large pine tree way up in the foreground, or show Mt. Fuji through the bottom of a large barrel that's being constructed. Those are dramatic compositions and I'm sure they had a strong effect on van Gogh. We consider this period when French painters were stuck in a rut to be a glorious time for the impressionists, but from the viewpoint of individual artists, ukiyo-e just happened to come along at a time when they were looking for a way to break out from what, to them, was stagnation.

Like you, I'm not dissatisfied with ukiyo-e itself, but I do find it disappointing that there is no early-modern Japanese art that you would want to, say, hang in the Palace of Versailles. Ukiyo-e certainly wouldn't be appropriate, but neither would the simple, refined tea bowls that Sen no Rikyū (1522–1591) so dearly loved. The gaudy colorfulness of Chinese porcelain would be much better suited, or a ceiling painting by an Italian artist. The culture of the Edo period is best enjoyed in a four-

and-a-half-tatami room. Not that that's a defect—it's just a characteristic.

Keene   Many foreigners who came to Japan in the early Meiji period collected Japanese antiques. But since they wanted to decorate large rooms—not the Palace of Versailles, but still sizeable— they were buying pieces of the poorest taste. They especially loved gaudy Satsuma ware, and of course the Japanese wanted to make the kind of things that they were after. Some foreigners just happened to buy tasteful items, but in most cases they sought out and purchased some really bad art.

Impressionists and artists of later periods did indeed love ukiyo-e. One Western tradition held that a person's face was in essence their soul, so you had to go to great pains to paint it well. That's one way that Western artists were stuck in a rut, because some faces are very interesting, but some just aren't. That can pose a problem if you're going to paint a portrait or something similar, but it's not a problem at all in the case of ukiyo-e. Faces in a Suzuki Harunobu (1725?–1770) ukiyo-e are Suzuki Harunobu faces. Every one looks the same. Even the men and the women have the same face—you have to look very carefully to determine which you're looking at. When you see a face in a Matisse painting, it has no features whatsoever. His faces serve no purpose.

Westerners had had enough of Rembrandts. They'd done what could be done in that direction, so they wanted to look at humanity from a different perspective. They decided it was okay to use a person as one element in a composition along with the other scenery, like in a kabuki play. Van Gogh copied one of Hiroshige's bridge pictures where all the faces are hidden by umbrellas. Being able to see their faces wouldn't make it a better picture. The people are only there to provide a convenient scale against which to measure nature, and to add a touch of humanity. That's quite different from the European tradition, in which human beings are at center stage and nature is the backdrop.

Two or three years ago, I went to see an exhibition in Naples of seventeenth-century Neapolitan paintings. Every one was of a human figure. The lack of nature was almost suffocating. It was just figure,

figure, figure… No nature at all. That's the European tradition.

Shiba That's an important point. Like, if the Spanish Crown had summoned Suzuki Harunobu and asked him to paint a portrait of the family of Carlos IV in the style of Francisco Goya (1746–1828), everyone would have ended up with the same face. [Laughs]

Keene I'd say Goya's approach was much more inconsiderate.

Shiba Just looking at the faces in Goya's *Charles IV of Spain and His Family* is enough to provoke a dramatic image of the fate of each person in that picture.

Keene Yeah, none of them have a pleasant expression, do they. [Laughs]

Shiba That might be the crux of the Western approach. It's what inspired Okakura Tenshin (1862–1913), along with Fenollosa and others, to start a new movement in painting in the first year of the Meiji period.

One of the main goals of that movement was, in my interpretation, to create Japanese paintings that you could hang in the Palace of Versailles. Another was to paint people. In the end, I don't think they were fully successful with the people. Or maybe they were? No, I don't think so, not under Tenshin's guidance, not fully. So that peculiarity of Japanese early-modern art—faces that are flat and expressionless—lasted well past the Meiji period. It's even around today.

Not to put down the artists, but when I visit Japanese art exhibitions I experience the opposite of what you felt in Italy. It drives me crazy, wondering why the artists don't reveal more of their subjects' humanness. The Japanese painter Uemura Shōen (1875–1949) was an exceptional painter. She painted things like a newlywed wife doing needlework, at precisely the moment when she successfully passes a thread through a needle. She captures the height of subtle tension in human motion. So it's beautiful, but I can't imagine that newlywed woman's fate. She does a good job of capturing that tension, which is rare in a Japanese artist, but she's so dominated by the traditional Japanese norm of painting things beautifully that she leaves the representation of human depth by the wayside. In that sense, even today—for better or worse—Japanese painting hasn't shaken off its early-modern inheritance.

Keene   A good example from the Muromachi period is the portrait of Ikkyū Sōjun (1394–1481). It's an amazing painting. You can read the man's life in his face.

Shiba   Right. I don't know how it's possible to paint a picture like that. When we see a face like that today, we think about how scary it would be to find that sort of old man lurking about. Those flared nostrils give him a somehow vulgar expression. Ikkyū was said to have been the illegitimate child of an emperor, but he seems so different there… No doubt it's a realistic depiction. His head isn't nicely shaved, it's all grown out.

Keene   His beard, too.

Shiba   That's right. Muromachi paintings were better than today's painters.

Keene   Watanabe Kazan (1793–1841) was another brilliant portrait artist. In the late Edo period, he painted Satō Issai (1772–1859) in this very realistic way that truly shows the kind of person Satō was. But most other painters of that era went straight for "beauty."

Shiba   I don't think Watanabe Kazan ever saw an oil painting by a Western painter. He studied Dutch, so he probably took an interest in the frontispieces of the Dutch books he read, and taught himself that kind of Western sketching. Those copperplate prints had a great deal of dimensionality, so his experience would have been the opposite of those French impressionist artists who were so shocked by the flatness of ukiyo-e. When you start painting with dimensionality, you're kind of forced to represent people as they are. So I think that Kazan was something of a special case.

Keene Dimensionality has a close association with sculpture, and Japanese sculpture is one of its greatest contributions to the art world. Sculpture from the Nara period, or maybe a little bit earlier, is particularly wonderful. But once you reach the early modern period, Enkū (1632–1695) is about the only artist making sculptures as grandiose and impressive as those Nara pieces.

Shiba That's true. You don't really see that kind of work after the capital was moved to Kyoto. I guess there was still some interesting sculpture for a time after the move, but around the end of the Heian period (794–1185), in the twelfth century, sculpture too starts to be all about beauty.

Folding Screens and Colorful Maps

Keene There were exceptions, though, like Unkei's (?–1223) *Niō* statues at the Great South Gate of the Tōdai temple.

Shiba Ah yes, the sculptors of Buddhist statues in Nara during the Kamakura period are a different story. Their sculptures have a sense of realism and dynamism. Representations of power like *Niō* statues are different from something like the statue of the monk Chōgen, which is just a countenance. They require an almost scary realism.

I have another theory about that. I think that the Kamakura shogunate of Minamoto no Yoritomo (1147–1199) was a government of peasants. Their samurai were something like the farmers in a cowboy Western. The Kyoto government decided that land belonged to the public, so individuals weren't allowed to freely do as they wished with it—though the government of course could. But the people rebelled against those laws, saying no, land that I farm is mine. So they farmed that land, and put on armor to protect it. Stronger people are better at protecting things, and the sculpture of the day reflected that spirit. Physical strength was the only way to protect the Kamakura shogunate. Besides that, Kyoto sculptors who had been crafting Buddhist figures for the Taira clan lost their jobs when the Kamakura shogunate arose, which may have provided new opportunities for Nara craftsmen like Unkei and Tankei (1173–1256) who had previously only been able to get jobs repairing Buddha statues from the Nara period.

The scroll paintings from that period are interesting, too. I love the ones of the monk Ippen (1239–1289) strolling about.

Keene I'm quite fond of those *Ippen hijiri-e* myself.

Shiba It's interesting that they don't just show Ippen walking alone. There are all these other people in the pictures—people working in rice paddies, even dogs. You don't see paintings like that in the early modern period. Paintings from the Kamakura period capture the entirety of humanity and nature, but in the early modern period it's all about prettiness.

Keene *Nanban* art was probably the last artistic movement in that tradition of capturing the entirety of humanity and nature. The nanban-style folding screens of Kanō Naizen (1570–1616) show not only dogs but also things like people doing handstands or fighting, and women selling things at stalls. The screens are fascinating because they show us what life was actually like at the time.

The paintings that include Portuguese people depict them a little differently from the Japanese, but they're still just another part of the scenery. There's no sense that they're fundamentally different from the Japanese. You can't even pick them out of the crowd if you don't look carefully. It's so interesting to look at them in that way, as just one element of the whole. I never get tired of looking at those paintings. But, as you say, once you get to the early modern period it's all about paintings being pretty.

Shiba The Kanō school started producing paintings in the days of Oda Nobunaga (1534–1582), but its artists were particularly active from the time of Toyotomi Hideyoshi (1536–1598) through the early Edo period. The bulk of their work was *rakuchū rakugai* screens depicting the scenery in and around Kyoto, which were in high demand among daimyo. Japan had already entered its period of isolationism, mind you, but the scenes they depicted had to have at least one Portuguese. That was quite a remarkable and valuable characteristic of those screens.

Some twenty years ago I purchased a rakuchū rakugai screen painted long after the early Edo period. I think it had once belonged to some temple, but it was still as beautiful as if it had been painted yesterday. I knew that if I kept it I wouldn't be able to maintain it in that condition, so after staring at the hundred or so figures depicted in it for a while, I resold it at the same price I paid for it. That screen, too, had many foreigners in it, so it was lots of fun to look at.

It's hard to imagine that the entire screen was painted by a single person, so I figure there must have been something like a big factory—well, a large studio I suppose—filled with apprentice painters helping to finish it. There were two or three hundred daimyo in Japan, and while these screens may not quite have been a de rigueur status symbol, they were very close, as was owning a Masamune *tantō* sword—a forgery, in most cases—and a Chinese painting by Muqi Fachang (1210?–1269?) imported during the Muromachi period. Fachang was a minor painter in China, but for some reason he was very popular in Japan, to the extent that a whole industry arose in the port city of Ningbo aimed at buyers from Japan. Most of the paintings on offer there were probably forgeries. Anyway, every daimyo wanted this set of three treasures, so rakuchū rakugai screen painters were kept quite busy. Those screens always included a foreigner, and where possible a colored person too.

Keene Servants and the like, right? The townsfolk, in turn, would buy portraits of actors, and people visiting Edo from the countryside would also return home with a souvenir ukiyo-e to show that they had seen a particular actor or kabuki play.

Shiba I'm sure that kept Edo ukiyo-e artists busy. Ukiyo-e were the prime souvenir for samurai, peasants, and townsfolk visiting Edo.

Artists also kept busy making *Edo kirie-zu* maps of the city. The Tokugawa shogunate required daimyo to spend every other year in Edo, and this brought tens of thousands of samurai to the city. These samurai would be sent out on errands, but unlike what you see in period films, daimyo, vassals, and samurai didn't put nameplates on their gates, so visitors had to rely on these beautiful colored maps to find them. When samurai completed their two- or three-year postings to Edo, the maps made a wonderful souvenir of their time in the capital. They weren't quite what you would call works of art, but they were a great way for folks to talk about that time granddad went to Edo and bought this map, or when dad went and bought this ukiyo-e. In a way they were a means for popularizing art among the early-modern masses.

Suki

Keene Aside from in the Heian court (794–1185), women's education didn't advance much until the early modern period. But then we start seeing people like Kaibara Ekken who viewed women's education as highly important. By the end of the Edo period most novel readers were women, and books were being written specifically to suit their tastes. Nothing like that took place before the early modern period. Books weren't a commercial product in the Heian period, but by the end of the Tokugawa shogunate they most certainly were. There was a strong sense that novels were something women bought. Part of that was due to the huge advancements in education for women and girls that took place during the Edo period.

Shiba   Book rental shops were a part of the urban culture of Kyoto, Edo, and Osaka. There was also a huge book rental shop called Daisō in Nagoya. Daisō even had academic books, but most of its customers were women. They would rent books from salespeople who travelled around the town carrying big stacks of books on their backs. You can't enjoy a book without being able to read, so it's a sign of how extensive education had become.

Keene   If you were to compare Japan and Europe in the early nineteenth century, I'm sure you'd find that Japan had a higher literacy rate and more extensive education. That's despite the fact that Japanese was written using kanji, and printed materials used cursive or semi-cursive variants for the kana, so they must have been awfully hard to read. But that didn't stop the Japanese from reading. When I look at books from that time, the writing looks like worm tracks—I can't read a thing. But people at the time apparently didn't have a problem with it.

Shiba   I suppose they learned those "worm-like" characters before they learned block writing. But anyway, yes, reading was very popular by the end of the Edo period. A bestseller from that time—among men, however, not women—was *Nihon gaishi* [An Unofficial History of Japan] by Rai San'yō (1780–1832). The bestseller at the very end of the Edo period was Fukuzawa Yukichi's *Seiyō jijō* [Things Western], which remained popular into the Meiji period. San'yō's history was unique in that it was a history of Japan, not China. Before that, reading history meant reading *Zuo zhuan* [Commentary of Zuo] or Sima Qian's *Shǐjì* [Records of the Grand Historian] or *Zizhi tongjian* [Comprehensive Mirror to Aid in Government]. It's almost like Japanese scholars of China never paused to think that their own country, too, had a history. Then along comes this complete history of Japan by Rai San'yō. Since the start of the Edo period, the Japanese had been fond of keeping records about fallen daimyo and the path by which their clans met their end during the Warring States period. All of these records provided San'yo with plenty of material to work from when producing a full history of Japan. That's quite a task, as you well know.[4]

Keene   It is indeed. [Laughs]

Shiba   Even the Chinese didn't have a complete history of China. I don't think one existed until Kuwabara Jitsuzō (1870–1931), the father of Kuwabara Takeo (1904–1988), wrote a textbook [first published in 1898] called *Chūtō tōyōshi* [Asian History for High Schools]. Anyway, there are no other complete histories of China, aside from those from ancient times. It seems that complete histories aren't something that people write about their own society. So first Kuwabara Jitsuzō writes his history of China, and that's followed by a second one, *Chūgoku no rekishi* [History of China], written by Kaizuka Shigeki (1904–1987) and published by Iwanami Shoten. And of course, you wrote the complete history of our literature. [Laughs] But anyway, the first history of Japan came in the late Edo period, in the form of Rai San'yō's *Unofficial History of Japan*, and if you read that you can learn everything up to the Edo period.

Now, San'yō approaches things from a Neo-Confucian perspective, so his account is very simplistic and doesn't have the kind of universal appeal that would make it interesting to, say, a Spaniard. But within Japan it was a huge bestseller that changed how people thought of their country. I don't think there was anyone who hadn't read it. Well, not every Japanese, but everyone interested in politics—and even if they hadn't read it themselves, they would have gotten an overview from someone else, because admitting to not having read it would have been very embarrassing. After that died down, *Things Western* came out, and again, just about everyone read it. The end of the Edo period was a heyday for reading, with women reading interesting novels and men finally starting to read books written in their own country.

---

4. Donald Keene is the author of a four-volume series, *A History of Japanese Literature*.

Keene   If you think about it, the popularity of San'yō's history shows that everyone back then could read classical Chinese.

Shiba   It does, doesn't it. The language he uses in *Unofficial History* is practically a foreign language.

Keene   It definitely is. It's not at all like Japanese.

Shiba   It's not, but San'yō writes in a form of classical Chinese that's somewhat Japanized. Scholars like Hoashi Banri (1778–1852) complained that by the standards of Chinese writing, San'yō's style was "shallow and reeks of Japanese." But the flip-side is that his writing was easy to understand, which allowed ordinary Japanese people to read it. I'm sure that any "reeking of Japanese" was wholly intentional. San'yō might have been more worried by Hoashi's criticisms had he been writing in the mid-Edo period, but in the late Edo he could proudly state that he was writing in a Japanese style because he was Japanese. Conversely, Professor Yoshikawa Kōjirō (1904–1980) praised San'yō's writing, citing an appraisal by the late Qing dynasty scholar Xian Tan (1832–1901). In any case, the fact that San'yō embraced a writing style that "reeks of Japanese" can't be unrelated to his trust in the cultural maturity of the late Edo period.

Keene   The Japanese held China in a certain reverence for many years. But in the mid-Edo some people started to take a more critical position, like Motoori Norinaga (1730–1801), and later on Hirata Atsutane (1776–1843). Hirata actually referred to the Chinese as "Western barbarians." [Laughs]

Shiba   How ridiculous. But I suppose it was overreach like that that gave San'yō his confidence.

Keene   That's probably true.

Shiba   There are many wonderful things about the Edo period, like how kabuki and sumo became stylized, but most wonderful of all is that cultural aspects like that weren't supported by the nobility, but rather by selling cheap tickets to commoners. I think that's a great way to describe the Edo period—as an era for the masses.

Sumo wrestling is basically something that children throughout the world do, but in the Edo period the Japanese made it into a show. Rules about not leaving the ring were codified to create a sport, and everything was turned into ceremony to delight the masses. Neither Korea nor China had a sport that energized the entire country in a similar way. I think one of the most significant features of the Edo period is that people were able to develop the economic basis for things like sumo and kabuki by selling cheap tickets to the masses.

Keene   Chikamatsu was a samurai, but when you read the jōruri and kabuki that he wrote, the most memorable thing is that the protagonists in his tragedies are townsfolk. Peasants and townsfolk sometimes appeared in European comedies, but it was a long time before they appeared in tragedies.

When we watch *Shinjū ten no amijima* [The Love Suicides at Amijima] today, we never lose sight of the fact that the paper merchant Jihei is a townsperson. His worst sin is that he neglects his business. Sure, he has a relationship with a prostitute, but that wouldn't have been a problem if he had done his job. His failure is that he lets his business suffer on account of this love affair with the beautiful Koharu, and the tragedy lies in the fact that he can't forget her. There would have been no tragedy if he'd done the common-sense thing, namely make money and spend an appropriate amount on his girl. But no, he forgets that he is first and foremost a merchant. That is his sin, which in the end leads to his dying with the woman that he loves. And that can only happen because Jihei is a townsperson. You couldn't put a samurai in that role.

Shiba This reminds me of discussions of *"suki"* [eccentric, possibly obsessive fondness for an artistic form] in the work of Hayashiya Tatsusaburō (1914–1998), a historian who as a young man investigated the history of medieval Japanese entertainment. Suki is a fundamental principle in forms of entertainment such as tea ceremony, but in the Muromachi period people found it frightening, because it could lead to one's downfall. A samurai who was overly obsessed with his tea ceremony implements might forget that he was supposed to be protecting his castle, for example. So to people back then, suki was the scariest word in Japanese.

Then in the Edo period, you see things like Jihei's fondness for Koharu leading to his downfall. In this case, the failure of his business is a measure of his love. I suppose people watching it at the time told themselves they should take care not to fall into the same trap, but at the same time they were probably a little jealous of someone experiencing suki to that extent.

Keene I'm sure they were. If Jihei and Koharu's story hadn't ended in suicide, I doubt anyone would remember them today. Like Romeo and Juliet, their end is what makes them memorable. I suppose that's something to envy.

Shiba So the Edo period warned against falling too deep into suki. The word actually became *dōraku* [debauchery] during that period, and being called a debaucher was the worst insult in the world of townspeople. Of course, even going to the theater on a regular basis was considered debauchery at the time.

Keene Novels written for townsfolk, like Saikaku's *Nippon eitaigura* [The Way to Wealth], were often about some prodigal son who wastes the wealth that his father struggled to accumulate, leading to the entire family's downfall…

Shiba And they fell so easily. I'm not sure if Saikaku was trying to warn us about how easily we can meet our end, or if he was praising his characters for plunging into suki to the extent that it destroys them. There's some ambiguity there.

Keene   There is indeed. In any case, he clearly wasn't angry with them. [Laughs]

CHAPTER 5
Japanese Language in Literature

Mother Tongues and Foreign Languages

Keene I recently visited Europe, and gave a presentation in French for the first time in twenty years.

Shiba That's quite some time. Did your French come right back to you?

Keene Most of it, yes. What surprised me most is that French words naturally came to me as I spoke. It was a very interesting experience.

Shiba I've heard that some seventy percent of English words come from French. Do poems containing lots of French-derived words feel stiff and formal, like Japanese poems with many Chinese-derived words do?

Keene Very much so. French is more a language of the head than the heart. It's a lot like the relationship between Japanese and Chinese. Japanese and English are similar in that way, in that they're both hybrids of other languages.

Shiba In daily speech, for example, it would sound gross if I said "I'm going to eat a cow" using the native Japanese term, but when I use the Chinese-derived word for "cow meat" instead, it doesn't sound bad at all. English does a similar thing, using words like "beef" and "mutton," right?

Keene   Exactly. Pork, too. All those words come from French. It would sound barbaric to say you ate cow.

Another similarity between English and Japanese is that both welcome words from other languages. That's particularly true of Japanese today, as you can see from all the advertisements filled with foreign words. In the case of English, it's long been considered classy to use French words. I lived in a university dormitory in England immediately after the Second World War. Those were hard times, so the food was really, really bad, but every day the menu was written in French. That didn't make it taste any better, but somehow having French names made it seem classier. [Laughs]

Shiba   French cuisine amidst destitution, huh. I suppose the development of the English language is related to its incorporation of foreign words.

Keene   Reaction to foreign words has varied with the times, but in general the affinity of English for loanwords is similar to that of Japanese. I guess it's possible to write in pure English or Japanese, using no words brought in from other languages, but it's very limiting to do so.

Shiba   In Japan's dynastic era, people like Murasaki Shikibu (c. 973–1014) had a good command of Chinese, which I imagine made them seem highly intellectual.

Keene   That's right. Today, trying to speak pure Japanese or pure English would make you sound very strange. In English, for example, we'd have to say "tonesmith" instead of "composer."

Shiba   I understand that you recently visited Belgium. I once spent two nights in Antwerp, thinking that it would be a convenient base for seeing Holland. When I was there I met a man from Amsterdam who told me the Dutch spoken in Antwerp sounded strange to him, because it still had equivalents to "tonesmith" for "composer." So apparently Dutch speakers in Antwerp aren't as fond of loanwords as are Dutch speakers in Holland.

Keene   That's because people in Holland don't feel they have to prove themselves as Dutch speakers. If you're living in Belgium, however, you're surrounded by French speakers, which causes this resistance to anything that seems counter to tradition—like speaking in anything other than pure Dutch. You'll get a cold reception if you try speaking French in Antwerp. Speak French in a shop there, and the clerk might ignore you. They'd rather lose a sale than have to speak French. [Laughs] You see things like that in Europe even today.

Shiba   The Dutch in Amsterdam and Leiden are very considerate, though. When a non-Dutch speaker like myself joins a meeting, they immediately switch to English, almost unconsciously. I think that shows how practical they are, and how they're not overly fixated on their own language.

Keene   I've also heard that at Dutch universities, if there's one American or British student in a class, the whole thing will be taught in English. Similarly, if there's a French or German student, the class is taught in their language. So I guess most Dutch speak four languages.

Shiba   I read in a book by Yoshikawa Kōjirō (1904–1980)—I think it was one of his, at least—that Hayashi Razan (1583–1657) communicated with missions from Korea by writing in Chinese. But he reportedly said they used words he didn't know. One of those words was apparently *women*, the Chinese word for "we," which you would normally learn in your first Chinese lesson. In other words, in the early Edo period, people like Hayashi Razan didn't know modern Chinese. He had studied under Fujiwara Seika (1561–1619), but both of them were largely self-taught individuals. They didn't have Chinese tutors to teach them the language, so they read it in this Japanese style that led them to not even knowing the word "we." I think this is highly symbolic of Japan's cultural isolation at the time. It would be like scholars from the same period trying to learn English but not knowing the word "we." Maybe the word *women* was a kind of slang at the time, but still…

Keene   When I first started teaching at Cambridge in 1948, British students learning Japanese would start with the introduction to the *Kokin wakashū* [Collection of Japanese Poems of Ancient and Modern Times]. British students traditionally also learned Latin, so there was some basis for starting with works from antiquity, even for Japanese. They studied language that wasn't really spoken, just like Latin. The introduction to *Japanese Poems* doesn't have much vocabulary, and it doesn't use much kanji, so I guess in that sense it was a rational choice, but the students couldn't speak a word of Japanese.

One day a student asked me what he should study over the summer holidays, and I recommended *Kagerō nikki* [The Gossamer Years]. There's a translation into modern Japanese, so I figured that if he didn't understand the original, he could consult that. When he came back from holidays I asked him how it had gone. He said he could understand the original work, but not a word of the modern edition. [Laughs]

Shiba   Sounds like another Hayashi Razan.

My friend Roger Machin graduated from the Japanese program at Cambridge in the 1960s, and he says that his first textbook was *Hōjōki* [An Account of My Hut]. He's really more interested in languages than in literature, but one day I learned something very interesting from him. I had proposed that he write an essay, which I would take to a newspaper publisher. He produced a manuscript, about four pages of four hundred characters each, but the only period in the entire thing came at the very end. When I told him it needed punctuation, he said that at Cambridge he had learned that Japanese was written as this long series of clauses, each linked to the next, with a single period to mark the end. Thankfully he acknowledged his misunderstanding when I told him that was the style from long, long ago.

Roger once told me something else that has continued to bother me. He said that one memorable thing they taught at Cambridge was that Japanese was all nouns. If you think about it—and expand the scope of what you consider a noun—Japanese can tie together a phrase using the word *koto* [thing] and treat it all as one big noun phrase. Then you just stick a *desu* [is] at the end, and you're done.

It made sense at the time, but the more I thought about it the stranger it seemed. I suppose that the instructors at Cambridge took a very broad interpretation of what a noun is. In any case, their instruction sounded very much like something out of classical education.

Keene I think things are very different now. The first Europeans who came to Japan and started learning Japanese—this would be at the end of the Muromachi period (1336–1573), a little before what we would call the early modern age—were people like the missionary João Rodrigues (1561–1633), who were young enough and mentally agile enough to pick up quite a bit of the language. Other people had a much harder time, though. At first they seemed to think that the grammar was similar to Latin, with the particles following Japanese nouns showing declensions. So you didn't just learn *ie* [house], you learned *ie ga* [the house specified], *ie no* [belonging to the house], *ie wo* [house as direct object], and *ie ni* [to the house] together with it.

Shiba Ah, I see. Very interesting.

Keene Much later, in the late Edo period, a French priest in Japan claimed that Japanese was invented by the Devil as a way to interfere with missionary work.

Shiba There was a seminary in Rome that taught a similar thing about the Basque language spoken in the Pyrenees mountains.

Keene   That's right. Same thing.

Shiba   Well I guess I should feel honored that the same consideration was paid to Japanese. [Laughs]

The Maturation of Written Japanese

Shiba   When would you say that everyone in England started writing in more or less what we consider English today?

Keene   Well, country folk had their own language, and still do, but if we're talking about literature, the language used in the early eighteenth century is pretty much the English we use today. Go back much further and you see words and expressions that modern speakers wouldn't understand, but by the eighteenth century the language was very similar.

Shiba   Charles Lamb wrote essays that were very similar to those by Japanese authors like Ozaki Kazuo (1899–1983) and Ibuse Masuji (1898–1993). Were there other writers before Lamb who wrote like that? Easy-to-understand descriptions of daily life, I mean.

Keene   It is not quite the same thing, but around the beginning of the eighteenth century people started writing essays for newly-established newspapers, and the language they used was very close to spoken language. It's like they were writing in prose rather than verse. In earlier times, even prose was written in hard-to-read language, sometimes even using words invented by the author. Writers proficient in Latin would just borrow from that if a word didn't exist in English. Today, their writing is hard to read without annotations. But that's not the case for writing from the early eighteenth century.

Shiba   I see. So I wonder if we can consider the eighteenth century as the period when all the main pieces of British culture—not just its literature—had emerged.

Keene Sure. Of course, there were dialects. Even today, I sometimes meet people I can't understand when traveling in England. Sometimes I don't even realize they're speaking English. Once I met someone who, after much consideration, I decided must be speaking a northern European language, but it turned out to be English.

But there aren't many people who write in dialect. Professional writers want to sell what they write, and you can't sell something that people can't read. In the past some literature was written for the lower classes, but I think that in most ways English was unified by the eighteenth century.

You can see this in English pronouns, for example. People used "thou" up until the eighteenth century, but you never hear that today. Well, maybe when addressing God in prayers and such, but otherwise we always say "you." At one time, both words were used for different purposes—"thou" was for people you were familiar with, and "you" was for others, like *tu* and *vous* in French, or *du* and *Sie* in German. But English today has dropped that.

Shiba Ah, interesting. So pronouns have caused problems even in English, like they did in Japan in the Meiji period (1868–1912).

Keene Japanese didn't even have them. [Laughs]

Shiba Japanese didn't need them, was the sentiment.

Keene Japanese honorific speech is enough to let readers know who you're speaking to. When you read the *jōruri* of Chikamatsu (1653–1725), if a woman is speaking you can tell whether she's speaking to her husband or a servant or a child, because she uses different language for each. But you don't hear a single pronoun.

Shiba The language is tricky. The Japanese pronouns *kimi* [you] and *boku* [I] appear to have emerged just before the Meiji Restoration among revolutionaries in Kyoto. In the Meiji period those terms became popular among students, particularly those at the law school in Kanda [Tokyo] and at Tokyo Imperial University [now the University of Tokyo]. But you wouldn't have heard them at your local barber shop, or at the florist—those folk probably never used *kimi* or *boku* in their entire lives. Those were essentially class-based words, which prevented them from being used by everyone at the time.

Keene   When you watch period films today, you often hear people calling each other *kisama* [you], which would be extremely offensive today, but was clearly a term of respect in olden days.

Shiba   If you consider the meaning of the kanji that word uses, it's excruciatingly polite.

Keene   It's hard to say whether Japanese has very few pronouns, or an extremely large number. For example, *ware* generally means "I," but in some regions it means "you."

Shiba   That's right, as a familiar term like *omae* in standard Japanese.

Keene   In some cases it's even a third-person pronoun, like in *ware wo wasureru* [to forget oneself] or *wagako wo mamoru* [to protect one's child]. In any case, it's interesting how quickly Japanese evolves.

Shiba   It is, isn't it.

Keene   For example, you almost never see the words *o-tōsan* [father] or *o-kāsan* [mother] in Meiji-period literature. Those are pretty basic words, but they're almost nonexistent there.

Shiba   Do you remember that time when we ran into each other at a ceremony at the Ise shrine, and went out drinking afterward? That night, you asked me when the words *o-tōsan* and *o-kāsan* entered Japanese, and that made me realize what a serious scholar you are. At the time I told you I thought it was probably during the early Meiji period, likely initiated by the Ministry of Education, but when I got back home and looked deeper into it, I found that the first use of those words in a textbook was around the turn of the century, in the third decade of the Meiji period. So, for example, Natsume Sōseki (1867–1916) likely didn't use those words when he was a child.

Not only did Natsume Sōseki produce great works as a novelist, he also contributed to the standardization of Japanese by writing in language that anyone could read. Before Sōseki we had writers like Izumi Kyōka (1873–1939) on the one hand, and on the other people like Yamaji Aizan (1864–1917) and Tokutomi Sohō (1863–1957), who were writing in a Japanese-style Chinese. Their styles were so different, it's hard to believe that something like Kyōka's *Uta andon* [A Song by Lantern-light] is from the same country. It's as if when the Edo period ended and the Meiji began, people wanted to wipe the slate clean, and part of that was creating a writing style for the new era. But I think it was all artificially cultivated.

Oh, and another interesting story: I've never studied German, so I asked a friend who's a German instructor for a one-minute description of what kind of language it is. His pithy description was, "It's the kind of language where no matter what you write, it sounds like a problem on a college entrance exam." Maybe that's characteristic of a language that has developed with a focus on grammar, but I take it as showing that German is a mature language. No matter your social position, your written German will be the same, which I consider a sign of the maturity of German society. Put another way, literary language can only mature when it is shared by all of its society.

Which leads to the question of when Japanese writing matured following the start of the Meiji period. I believe that we see the first mature use of the language with Natsume Sōseki. It's mature in the sense that it's versatile—you can use the same language to write about Japan–U.S. trade friction or to write a novel describing your attitudes towards romantic emotion—and Sōseki created it around the fortieth year of the Meiji period [1907]. Others continued that effort in various ways in the early Shōwa period (1926–1989).

Take for example the minor writer Kataoka Teppei (1894–1944). In 1925 he wrote a book called *Shin-kankaku-ha wa kaku shuchōsu* [A Proclamation of the New Sensationalists] that today is completely unreadable, the writing is so rough. [Laughs] But Kataoka also wrote novels for the masses, and those are written in a very approachable style. It's only when he's making political arguments, or when he's writing about what the sensationalist movement is all about, that he uses such a grandiose style that it's hard to understand what he's trying to say.

Sōseki created a much more versatile writing style that anyone could adopt, but it didn't quite take root. I once asked the French literary scholars Kuwabara Takeo (1904–1988) and Kawamori Yoshizō (1902–2000) when it was that Japanese matured to the level of language that you'd see in college entrance exams or final exams at universities like Bonn or Paris-Sorbonne or Columbia. They both took several days to reply, and gave different answers. Kawamori said it was around 1952 or 1953, while Kuwabara said 1958. Kuwabara mentioned 1956 as the year when *Shūkan shinchō* was launched. That periodical had quite advanced content—for a weekly news magazine at least—and a circulation in the hundreds of thousands, so it had to appeal to a broad audience. That's why he considers that to be the period in which Japanese matured.

In any case, I still think it was Sōseki, well before that, who first created a literary Japanese that anyone could enjoy. What do you think?

Keene When I'm reading Edo-period literature I occasionally run into a very modern-sounding expression, which is kind of a thrill. Even in the jōruri of Chikamatsu, or in popular *gesaku* literature, you sometimes see a turn of phrase that wouldn't be out of place if used by people today.

But indeed, a new Japanese developed in the time of Sōseki, particularly in his own writings. Futabatei Shimei's (1864–1909) *Ukigumo*

[The Drifting Cloud] is said to be the first novel to use colloquial language, but it is definitely not the Japanese of today. Not that it's strictly literary language, but it's like the Japanese of the late Edo period with some modern expressions tacked on. That's my take on it, at least.

When I read Edo-period literature from before Sōseki's time, I usually can't generate a clear image of what's being written about. As a poor parallel, for example, calligraphy that anyone can read isn't necessarily good calligraphy. There's even some respect paid to very difficult pieces that hardly anyone can read. Or sometimes you visit a café with some movie actor's autograph up on the wall, and it's written in characters that are impossibly hard to read. It's considered "artistic." If it was written in simple, highly legible characters, you might not bother putting it up on the wall.

You see ornamental elements like that in Edo-period literature. With Chikamatsu, sometimes these elements make the meaning more complex, but more often they just make his writing prettier. When people listen to jōruri they don't necessarily understand what the words mean, but they get a sense of the mood—that the speaker is sad, or depressed or whatever. That makes analysis very difficult, though. Something like Chikamatsu's *michiyuki* becomes extremely difficult. It makes me wonder if anyone listening at the time could really understand it.

Shiba   I feel the same way.

Keene   I suppose that so far as the general audience was concerned, they got the general point that these two young lovers committed suicide together, and that was enough.

But when we get to Sōseki in the Meiji period, they understood the whole thing. There's nothing ornamental there—it's all about content and expression. In other words, language is being used for a different purpose. Previously it had been used in a more multifaceted way, to create beauty along with some modicum of meaning. In contrast with earlier Japanese writers who just wanted to produce beautiful words, Sōseki and later writers seem to be trying to impart something to the reader. I'm not sure why one would consider 1958 such a significant year, though.

Shiba   Nor am I. Professor Kuwabara seems to have brought up the golden age of weekly periodicals due to a personal experience related to the geophysicist Nishibori Eizaburō (1903–1989). In 1957, Nishibori was captain of the wintering party for the first Japanese Antarctica exploration team. Kuwabara and Nishibori attended high school together and were friends, though Nishibori went into the sciences. When Nishibori returned from Antarctica, Kuwabara told him that he should write a book recounting his experiences—that Europeans and Americans who experienced something rare would report on it to society, and he should do the same. Nishibori refused, using the typical Japanese excuse of the day that he was a scientist, not a writer. "Not a problem," Kuwabara said. "You're commuting from Kyoto to Osaka City University every day, so just read *Shūkan asahi* on the train." *Shūkan asahi* started publication at the end of the Taishō period (1912–1926), before *Shūkan shinchō*, but anyway Kuwabara gave him the name of a weekly periodical, and after reading it for a few months Nishibori was able to write in that style.

In other words, Kuwabara knew that these weeklies were written in a language that anyone could appreciate, so that's probably why he mentioned them in response to my question. But probably the reason for him saying *Shūkan shinchō*, instead of *Shūkan asahi*, was that while previously only newspaper companies were publishing weekly periodicals, starting in 1956 all the publishing companies had one, so now they were everywhere, with huge circulations. That's when we first saw this flood of publications in language that anyone could understand.

Keene   I think it was sometime around 1890 that Ozaki Kōyō (1867–1903) became very concerned with whether he should write in a literary style or a colloquial one. On the one hand, he thought that as an artist he should use a literary writing style, because anyone could write in a colloquial style and that meant it wasn't artistic. Japan had this wonderfully artistic language, he thought, and it shouldn't be abandoned.

I can understand that. When you write Japanese in the old style, you're carrying on a tradition from a thousand years ago. So there's this tradition, and you want your words to have a certain tone that will resonate with the emotions of people from long ago.

Then again, Ozaki also considered the modern era to be a prosaic one, so he used contemporary language in novels like *Aobudō* [Green Grapes]. In the end, though, he wrote *Konjiki yasha* [The Usurer] in a literary style. He felt that as a professional writer, he must write like a professional. An amateur, a scientist like Nishibori Eizaburō, could write whatever they wanted, but as a professional he seemed to consider it embarrassing to use such simplistic language.

Shiba   I think that tradition stretches all the way back to the Edo period. In the case of Ozaki Kōyō, I think he probably learned to create beautiful prose by practicing with classical language. Interestingly, Izumi Kyōka was from Kanazawa and so he only knew the Kaga dialect. When he came to Tokyo he wanted to write novels that sounded like they came from Tokyo, but he wasn't sure what to base that on. Rather than take more traditional routes to learning how to write, he started going to *rakugo* comic storytelling theaters, and based his language on what he heard there. I think that's a good example of how people in the Meiji period wove together this new language.

I think Sōseki was able to take things to the next level because he had struggled with the English language while he was studying in England, which made him stop to consider what language is, and to reconsider Chinese-style composition and old-style Japanese like haiku. In the end he just threw up his hands and published his first novel, *Wagahai wa neko de aru* [I Am a Cat], in a haiku magazine. There were probably other magazines around that were put together by literary groups, but publishing through a haiku magazine allowed him to take a more carefree approach to his writing.

I once read something interesting, written by a student in the old junior high school system during the Taishō period. His Japanese

teacher had made the class memorize and recite the opening passage to
Gubijinso [The Poppy], which had just been published in the *Asahi
shimbun* newspaper. It wasn't an especially literary work, but it was
new. If we read that story today it feels very old-fashioned, particularly
for something by Sōseki, but from the perspective of a Taishō-period
Japanese teacher it apparently felt quite new and different, to the point
that he had his students memorize it. That was quite surprising to me,
this preconceived notion that anything by Sōseki must be "new." I
mean, the opening to *The Poppy* isn't very good.

Keene   No, it isn't. If you consider the works by Mori Ōgai (1862–
1922) from the same time, he clearly doesn't want to write in a colloquial style, though in the end he seems to give in to it. He seems to believe
that he has to protect historical kana usage. Other writers in the Taishō
period were giving up old styles and using a reformed, easier-to-read
way to write Japanese, but Ōgai stood against that. He just couldn't
bring himself to do it. That's how much he loved old literature. He may
have studied in Germany and been influenced by romantic literature,
but he thought of Japanese as something different.

Shiba   Right. Like you were saying before, people in the Edo period
considered difficult sentences and phrasings that uncultured people
wouldn't understand as the sign of professional work, and that carried
over to some Meiji-era writers.

When I received the Naoki Award in 1959, Fujisawa Takeo—a man
some twenty years older than me from a family of Confucian scholars
stretching back to the Edo period—gave me a hanging scroll as a con-
gratulatory gift. It's a small one painted by Takizawa Bakin (1767–
1848). I still keep it as a valued treasure, but I have no idea what it says.
Although it's written in block script rather than cursive, it has a character that Bakin seems to have invented himself— at least, it wasn't in the
dictionary when I tried to look it up. Mr. Fujisawa says he thinks it
might mean "no falsehoods," which is interesting considering that
Bakin is known for the anecdotal work *Nansō satomi hakkenden* [The

Eight Dog Chronicles].

In any case, there does seem to have been an attitude that professionals wrote in a way that was hard to understand, or drew characters that were hard to read.

Keene You can even say the same thing about Nagai Kafū (1879–1959). He was enamored with the atmosphere of decadent eras like the late Edo, and he tried to produce a similar atmosphere in his writing.

When he first encountered naturalist writing, he didn't consider it literature. He even said he couldn't understand the writings of his contemporary Masamune Hakuchō (1879–1962). The books by naturalists like Masamune aren't difficult at all—they're written in Japanese that anyone can understand. So I get the feeling that Nagai is putting on airs, pretending to not understand differences in how certain words used to be used versus how they're used now. I think he believed that professional writers wouldn't deign to use such rough language, or was even pretending that he wouldn't understand it.

Journey to the Classics

Keene Learning Japanese as a foreigner is very difficult, but when I read classical literature I'm glad that I put in the effort. A Japanese learner who ended up majoring in politics or economics would never know the joy it can provide. To them, Japanese is just a means to an end, a way to be able to read various things or get a good job. But a student who can read the classics is able to truly appreciate the beauty and pleasure of Japanese. That has been the most satisfying thing for me as a teacher. I definitely felt that way the year we read Chikamatsu's *Meido no hikyaku* [The Courier for Hell]. My students all said they enjoyed it too.

Shiba I can see how a work like that would excite them.

Keene   It did. It's hard to engage in literature that you rush through, so students read something like that very, very slowly. But Chikamatsu's work remains interesting even at that pace—the quality remains even when you read slowly, or when while translating it into English. Part of what makes it interesting is that it's not solely a tragedy—it's a drama that also has elements of humor and irony. Of course, *The Courier for Hell* isn't the only work like that.

Shiba   That's why the classics are important.

Keene   There are two approaches you can take when teaching Chikamatsu. You can approach him as a phenomenon of the Edo period, or you can treat his jōruri as an element in the history of Japanese theater. I tend to emphasize the latter. For example, I teach about the relationship between his jōruri and noh or older forms of jōruri, and about how his successors modified his classic works. If you try to teach it from the perspective of Japanese history or the history of the Edo period, it just takes too long. Plus, other courses cover that material, so I can leave it up to those instructors. In an ideal world I would teach it from both perspectives, but there's just not enough time.

Shiba   Understanding things against a cultural backdrop is difficult. Like, you know how we read translated novels in our teens and came away not quite understanding them, but feeling like we did? It's a completely different experience to reread those books in your fifties, when you know something about Europe. Not that it isn't fun to read in ignorance.

Keene   That's right. But if you think about it, it's hard to believe that Edo-period prostitutes all had the hearts of gold that Chikamatsu depicts. Surely some of them were just in it for the money. And the men, too, can't have all been such upstanding gentlemen. There have to have been some jerks. That's just the way the world is. But reading Chikamatsu, we're able to set that knowledge aside and assume that everyone is just as he presents them. I mean, the play just doesn't work if we consider that maybe Chūbei had another woman stashed away somewhere.

Shiba A nice example of when you don't necessarily need background.

I don't give many talks, but I did give one once to the Japanese department at your alma mater, Cambridge, and that's one of my fondest memories. When I speak to British people I feel like I need to throw in a bit of humor and wit, and everyone there kindly responded to the bad jokes I made every couple of minutes. I know I should probably keep my language as simple as possible, but sometimes I just don't have the right words. For example, when talking about differences in Meiji literature I compared Izumi Kyōka and Tokutomi Sohō, starting out saying "Izumi Kyōka's writing is…" and, unable to find a better description, ended that with "flabby." Everyone surprised me by bursting out in laughter.

The audience were all students of foreign language, and their sensitivity with regards to it was very impressive. I don't think there's ever been more interest in foreign languages and foreign ways of thought. In a sense, the world has become one. There are few truly unique places. We Japanese tend to think of ourselves as unique, but from a global perspective we're just like everyone else.

Even so, I suppose we're searching for something unique about our culture. There's nothing like *The Courier for Hell* in the theater of other countries, for instance, so I suppose people find that very interesting today. We can point to it as something distinctive when explaining Japanese literature and culture, but I guess in other places there are similarities. If you search hard enough, you can find the parallels between countries.

Keene Something I love about reading the literature of the past is discovering that even long ago there were people similar to yourself, and also reading extremely vivid descriptions of people. This may not be a very good metaphor, but when you look at photographs of Japanese people from the Meiji period, everyone is expressionless. If there's one person among ten or fifteen who's smiling, that person looks so very alive. You think, ah, so there were people like this, and you feel a closeness akin to friendship.

In the same way, for example, you read in *The Courier for Hell* about all of these stupid things that Chūbei does. He exemplifies the saying "haste makes waste," always getting angry and doing bad things. But you never struggle to understand him. Anyone could have acted the same way. We all know that his stealing and using the money will result in his death, but he has this extraordinary humanness to him. Reading *The Courier for Hell*, you can't help but feel close to him—despite the temporal and physical distance, you know that he's a human being, just like you.

Shiba   Right, it isn't hard to imagine someone entrusted with delivering cash just taking it and using it for himself. I suppose that universality is what made Chikamatsu such a big deal in his time.

Keene   When you read foreign literature, especially the literature of countries very different from your own, it's always fun to encounter things that don't exist in your own culture. But by far the more important thing is universality, and gaining a sense of how others are human too, just like you.

There's a scene in Shakespeare's *Julius Caesar* where Caesar is walking with Mark Antony, and Caesar asks him to walk on his right side, because he's deaf in his left ear. That feels like such a twentieth-century thing to say. It's a minor thing, but it makes the scene feel more alive.

Shiba   That's right. It's conversations and scenes like that that fill out the people being depicted. Those little quirks make you feel closer, but you don't see them in Meiji-period photographs, do you.

You once wrote something that really moved me, about the stone monument that Basho saw at the Taga castle in Miyagi prefecture when he visited there. Somewhere along the way people tend to pick up the idea that nature is forever, while words are fleeting and ephemeral. But the interesting thing about Bashō is that he considered nature to be empty and the words we write to be everlasting. The monument evoked that feeling in him. I had never encountered that kind of outlook before. Bashō loved nature, but he considered words expressing the human spirit to be even more important.

Keene   That's right. That's what most impressed me when reading his *The Narrow Road to Oku.*

Shiba   I hadn't picked up on that over many years of reading it.

Keene   Bashō was an admirer of the Tang dynasty poet Du Fu. He quotes a line from Du Fu, "The country is destroyed; yet mountains and rivers remain," but if you think about it that isn't necessarily the case. Mountains erode, and rivers change course. So what does remain? Human words. Human writing. Not only our writing, I suppose, but for example if we visit Egypt we don't really care what kind of trees or mountains used to be there. It's the hieroglyphics left behind by humans left that thrill us.

Shiba   Right. In the Kisakata region of Akita prefecture there's a place called the Kanman temple that today is up on a small hill, but in Bashō's time the sea was higher so it was an island. When Bashō visited it he wrote a haiku that went "Kisakata— Seishi sleeping in the rain, wet mimosa blossoms," comparing this inlet in Akita prefecture to a beautiful woman from Chinese mythology. When you look at the scenery in Kisakata it's not really all that impressive, but there's something about that haiku that really adds to it.

Keene   It really does. If Bashō hadn't written about the place, I doubt that trains would even stop there. [Laughs] But it's not just the haiku. It's also described in *The Narrow Road to Oku,* so when you visit you can visualize the place through Bashō's eyes. That's important. If you visit without knowing anything about *The Narrow Road to Oku*, then you have to rely only on your own eyes, and all you see in Kisakata are bumpy little hills amidst lots of fields.

Shiba   That Taga castle monument moved me very deeply, and as you said its continued existence really moved Bashō as well. Actually, I visited it again at New Year's the year before last, and of course recalled all that. Funnily enough, the only thing written on the monument itself is the distance to other places and things like that.

Keene   The actual writing isn't interesting at all. [Laughs]

CHAPTER 6

The Japanese and the Absolute

Absolute Gods and Fiction

Shiba There's something I'd like to ask you about.

We Japanese—and Koreans and Chinese as well—have a problem understanding Western concepts of the "absolute."

Specifically, it's hard to understand how there can simultaneously be this world of relative existence or nonexistence, alongside a world that includes an absolute. Space and the earth are relative worlds, as is science. There's nothing absolute in science. But when something transcends science—well, not just science, but anything that's relative—it's hard to understand.

Of course, in the thirteenth century you had people like Shinran (1173–1263) talking about "the way of absolute uniqueness," and later Nishida Kitarō (1870–1945) writing about "the self-identity of absolute contradictions," but I understand absolutism in those cases. They don't have anything to do with the creation of the world, or condemning people.

Put simply, I'm talking about the God of Christianity. It's hard to understand an entity that's transcendent and absolute, and also a creator. Not hard to understand in religious terms, of course, but philosophically.

The Judeo-Christian world has considered God absolute since ancient times. But there's nothing like that in Japan, or other parts of East Asia. "Heaven" in Confucianism is just a minor notion, not an absolute. If you don't understand this "absolute," a lot of other things don't fall into place.

Not that I'm putting down Japanese culture or literature, but for example when I read Camus or Dostoevsky, I think, we Japanese could never have written something like that. The era of God was over—well, not for Dostoevsky, but definitely by Camus' time—but even Camus was affected by some kind of residual cultural heat related to the absolute.

From a Japanese perspective, which is to say a pantheistic one, we're quick to consider the absolute a lie, even as we're giving offerings at an *inari* shrine. Western theologians have been developing arguments for the existence of God for millennia, along with related philosophies. Or they adopted such philosophies. Camus emerged as a writer after that work was finished, but he continued the business of creating new fictions.

I consider what he created to be Fiction with a capital "F," in the same sense as God with a capital "G." In other words, writers started considering Fiction an absolute, in the same way that theologians considered God an absolute. Literary problems were developed by placing Fiction at the core, something that you only rarely see in Japan.

In the Taishō period, something called the "I novel" appeared. I'm a huge fan of Ozaki Kazuo (1899–1983) and Shiga Naoya (1883–1971), and even of relatively minor authors like Kawasaki Chōtarō (1901–1985). Reading them gives me such peace of mind. It's a pantheistic kind of peace, like when you're walking in a valley and find a shrine to that valley's *kami* amidst the overgrowth.

But I don't really consider "I novels" to be novels in the modern literary sense because, simply put, there's no absolute Fiction in them.

I guess I'm blathering on a bit, not really asking you a question so much as talking to myself.

I think Mishima Yukio (1925–1970) may have picked up on that. But in his case, since there's no concept of the absolute in Japan—no absolute that is necessarily universal to humanity—he made the emperor an absolute according to his sensibilities. I sometimes wonder if

Mishima was the only one who noticed that. And perhaps because he noticed it he felt he had to resolve it, though he did so in his own peculiar way.

I'm particularly fond of Ozaki Kazuo's short story *Mushi no iroiro* [Entomologica], but I suppose that a Westerner would consider that to be an essay.

Keene   It is an essay.

Shiba   But from a Japanese perspective, it's a kind of short story. Because Ozaki writes fiction! [Laughs]

I definitely want the world to appreciate Japanese literature—and you've done a lot toward that end—and as part of that, I sometimes wish that "I novels" like *Entomologica* would be considered fiction.

Not to repeat myself, but in Europe you had God, and just as that tradition started weakening, modern literature arose. Writers started presenting their own absolutes, and making them central to their fiction.

But there's no absolute here in Japan, this pantheistic world where there are kami in the mountains and the valleys and the streams, even in the breeze. That's the climate in which the "I novel" was born.

Buddhism is another part of it. The emptiness that Buddhism holds to be the only truth is a relative state, even though it's unique. Zen Buddhism equates salvation with attaining emptiness, and the Jōdo Shinshū sect of Shinran names that emptiness the Buddha Amida [Amitābha] and gives it thanks. "Emptiness" isn't transcendent in a Christian sense, nor is it a Creator. For that reason, it's much more comfortable to us.

So I guess my point with all this is that when it comes to modern literature, the customs of Japan are a little off-kilter. Or maybe I'm just babbling.

Keene   I love early modern literature, starting with my personal focus on Chikamatsu. I don't think that he had any intention of inserting his personal beliefs into his *jōruri*. Saikaku (1642–1693) certainly didn't. For him, literature was a kind of play. He wrote about eroticism, and townsfolk, and all kinds of other things, but he clearly wasn't trying to do the same thing that, say, Dostoyevsky was.

If you want to find Japanese literary works similar to those of Europe, I think you have to go to Bashō (1644–1694). He wrote in this extraordinarily short poetic form of haiku, but I feel like he put his all into them. In that sense he's different from other poets. I also like Buson (1716–1784), but I don't feel that he puts his entirety in his haiku. Some of his haiku are very interesting, but there aren't many that evoke deep feelings.

Speaking of the absolute, in Japanese religion there's the Shintō tradition of countless kami, and then Buddhist concepts like *honji suijaku*, which poses that those countless kami embody different avatars of the Buddha, so the two traditions don't really conflict. On the other hand, Buddhists believed in *aji honpushō*—the idea that the world has always existed—while Shintōists believe that the world was created by Izanagi and Izanami stirring up the oceans to create some islands. In that way, Buddhism and Shintō contradict each other. Or regarding the question of what follows death, Buddhism says that if you were good you attain nirvana or become a bodhisattva or something, while Shintō says that you just decompose.

Shiba   Right, there's no afterlife in Shintō.

Keene   There are other contradictions between Shintō and Buddhism too, but the Japanese have found ways to weave them together. Hirata Atsutane (1776–1843) is a somewhat peculiar example of that. He picked up many ideas from reading Chinese translations of Christian texts, and he wanted to create a single God, Musubi-no-kami, to present as the focus of Shintō. He never even touched upon Amaterasu.

Shiba   Hirata wanted to cast Ame no minakanushi, a god that appears just once at the beginning of the *Kojiki* [Records of Ancient

Matters], as the Supreme Being.

Keene   Right. I believe that shows how strongly Christianity influenced him. But beliefs like that did not last. None of Hirata's followers believed anything like that, and nothing similar appears in his later works. He hated Buddhism, but Shintō alone proved insufficient to resist it. He could use Christianity to attack Buddhism, though, so I suppose in that sense it held some attraction for him.

Anyway, the Japanese recognize the possibility of countless kami, which makes it easier for them to see things in relative rather than absolute terms. The language reflects that too, for instance in the frequent Japanese use of words like "probably."

Shiba   Japanese avoids decisiveness. It prefers to stay vague and see how things turn out.

Keene   Westerners want to hear a "yes" or a "no," and if it's a "probably" then we want to know how probably. But the Japanese view obfuscation as part of the language. I've heard the phrase "if it isn't clear, it isn't French," but in the case of Japanese it's more like "if it's clear, it isn't Japanese." Japanese doesn't want to draw clear lines, saying "this is good" and "this is bad."

Shiba   We also use "one can believe" a lot, without stating who would believe it.

Keene   And "not necessarily not." [Laughs]

Shiba   Japanese avoids clarity of features, clarity of mass, and clarity of essence. The West derives clarity from its roots in the absolute, but vagueness is at the core of Japan, for example in the concept of emptiness and the various kami. Vagueness is widely understood to be essential to peace, and that may have directed the development of Japanese.

To build on your point about honji suijaku, it developed in the tenth and eleventh centuries as "fiction" with a small "f," but I think its development shows great talent in the Japanese. This massive system of Buddhism had come in and was destroying the Japanese gods, so I think of honji suijaku as a fiction that brought those gods back to life. It put Buddhist deities at the top, and Japanese gods beneath them, but this allowed "native" [*honji*] buddhas to "manifest" [*suijaku*] as kami. That keeps both the kami and the buddhas happy.

At the Ise shrine, for example, the native buddha Vairocana—well, really it's native to India, I suppose—but its manifestation within Japan appears as Amaterasu. It allows us to consider Vairocana and Amaterasu as one and the same. There's even a Buddhist convent at the Ise shrine, Keikōin. The Yasaka shrine in Kyoto was actually also a Buddhist temple, one that was forced to convert during the Meiji period. In the past you would have seen monks chanting sutras in worship. The enshrined deity at the Yasaka shrine is Susanoo no mikoto, who equates to Gozu Tennō in Buddhism.

In this way, honji suijaku, the combination of kami and buddhas, was a great accomplishment—if we can praise it like that—by the Japanese of the tenth and eleventh centuries. A talent not unlike a talent for appeasing conservative party fixers, maybe, but I suppose it appeased the countless kami of Shintō. That's why I think it was a mistake for the Meiji government to try to separate the kami and the buddhas in their efforts to establish Shintō as the national religion. As a result, many shrines lost precious treasures and statues. It was a terrible loss.

But setting that aside, Shintō for example has no satisfactory answer to the question of what happens after you die, so it's a little different. It isn't really a religion in the normal sense. Religions have founders and scriptures and doctrines, but Shintō has none of those things. It finally got established as a religion through syncretism, but when the Meiji government stripped Buddhism from it, it was forced to walk alone. And it's still walking alone today.

I'm a big fan of Shintō—as you can tell from the fact that we bumped into each other at the dedication rite at the Ise shrine, which takes place every twenty years—but I think we have to consider post-Meiji Shintō as something distinct. Post-Meiji Shintō was created by Hirata Atsutane's followers, as you just said. In the Meiji period the Department of Divinities was established to separate Shintō and Buddhism, but most of its members weren't actual Hirata devotees, so we ended up with State Shintō. Hirata followers would have created a more thoughtful, or at least a more universal religion. Hirata was left alone in post-Meiji Shintō, without a seat at the table. In any case he created, well, not an absolute god but a supreme god, and he developed a cohesive philosophy, so I agree with what you said.

Japan's religious life is complex and vague, just like its language. We have Shintō wedding ceremonies and Buddhist funerals, and Japanese is just as ambiguous.

Mishima Yukio and Kiyozawa Manshi

Keene You said that Mishima Yukio was after something absolute, and I agree. He professed the infallibility of the emperor, but I don't think he had the Emperor Shōwa or Emperor Meiji in mind—he was thinking of a more abstract emperor.

Shiba Sure.

Keene Mishima believed that his abstract, absolute emperor could never err. That any other kind of world would be meaningless. He thought that if everything were relative, if the Japanese emperor were the same as the British queen, then the world was without meaning.

His last four novels were a series called *Hōjō no umi* [The Sea of Fertility], which is somewhat ironic. The "Sea of Fertility" that he's referring to is on the moon, and it has no water. It's just a name. I think that when Mishima viewed the world, he saw something similar—a nihilistic world of nothingness. If there was anything at all, it was his abstract notion of the emperor. You can call that God if you prefer, but Mishima didn't believe in God, just in the existence of his abstract emperor.

He also wrote a novella called *Eirei no koe* [Voices of the Heroic Dead], in which kamikaze pilots denounce the emperor's declaration that he was a mortal being following the Second World War. If the emperor is merely human, they said, then what did we die for? Mishima thought that in the absence of the absolute, the sacrifices of Japan's war heroes were all in vain. But I guess the tragedy of Mishima was that in the end, he was unable to believe anything whatsoever.

Shiba   I think Mishima Yukio used the word "kami" with a particular meaning, one that differed from kami like *inari* fox gods or the kami of the Yasaka shrine. His kami were more like a big-"G" God. Like you say, Mishima wasn't a Christian, so his search for the absolute led him to the emperor. But it wasn't any specific emperor—what he grabbed onto was his concept of an absolute emperor. He thought he couldn't write without that. He thought of the emperor more as literature than as an ideal, but that's not something I can really comprehend. It's something I'd have to talk to him about face-to-face, but I get the feeling that you have a better understanding of it. He must have been enamored with the absolute.

Keene   I believe so.

Shiba   Unfortunately, however, you won't find that in Japan.

Keene   That's the case in Mishima's *Kinkakuji* [The Temple of the Golden Pavilion] as well. In that work, the Golden Pavilion was the absolute, and so long as it existed, the protagonist Mizoguchi could never be free. He couldn't love a woman as long as this absolute beauty lay before him. It shows Mishima's extreme yearning for the absolute.

Shiba   I see. I visited the Golden Pavilion as a reporter after it burned. I was on the night shift, and just went as part of my job. So for me, the Golden Pavilion is a very relative world. [Laughs]

Keene Long after that I read Mizukami Tsutomu's (1919–2004) *Kinkaku enjō* [The Burning of the Golden Pavilion], which is how I learned just how uninteresting the monk who burned it down was. But if you read Mishima's book, as a reader you can't help but feel sorry for the guy—you can understand how destruction of the absolute was necessary for his release.

Shiba Now that's an interesting literary theory. The monk who set the fire was named Hayashi Yōken, and for me he was a real, specific person. Mizukami interviewed me about what kind of person Hayashi was, and I gladly told him. He took notes and created a fictional world from them. Mishima turned it into a problem of the absolute. I guess the three of us are nothing alike. [Laughs]

I follow the Jōdo Shinshū sect of the Hongan temple, so I'd like to talk a bit about the Japanese concept of an "absolute" god, from the perspective of its adherents.

Hirata Atsutane developed a supreme god on his own, but Shinran set forth Amitābha as the absolute being. At least, that's the impression I get from reading his *Tannishō* [Lamentations of Divergences].

I wonder, though, if believers in the Edo period actually felt the same way. I'm not sure on that point. In analyzing Shinran, it seems that belief in Amitābha as an absolute being emerged as a philosophy after the Meiji period.

Kiyozawa Manshi (1863–1903) was born into a family of Owari-domain *ashigaru* foot-soldiers belonging to the Higashi-hongan temple. The temple paid for his education at Tokyo Imperial University, where he studied the philosophy of Hegel and interpreted Shinran from that perspective. Hegel had that belief in the absolute, and Kiyozawa developed a new teaching based on Shinran's belief in the absoluteness of Amitābha.

Around 1948, I asked a monk at the Hongan temple if paradise really existed, and he answered "It lies beyond questions of its existence." As far as absolutes go, I think that's pretty much a perfect answer. If you asked a Catholic priest if God really existed, I would expect the same answer. So I think this kind of thought among Jōdo Shinshū adherents began with Kiyozawa.

When noted Marxist Kamei Katsuichirō (1907–1966) was released from prison in the early Shōwa period (1926–1989) he became deeply absorbed in Shinran's teachings. Marx, too, put the absolute fiction of historical inevitability at the center of his work. Marx himself might be the result of theology, in that he represents the point of divergence between the theologies and philosophies developed in Europe.

At the risk of straying too far from the topic of philosophy, there are a lot of similarities between the Communist Party and groups like the Society of Jesus, or the Franciscans, or monastic groups, don't you think? I mean, the greatest suffering of the Jesuits and the Franciscans and the Salesians and the like is their absolute submission to orders. Marx didn't create the Communist Party, but it developed out of his work, and I think it really resembles these religious orders.

To escape from Marxism after he left prison, Kamei Katsuichirō adopted Japanese ideas of the "absolute" in the form of Shinran's teachings, though I suspect they functioned more as a form of sedative for him than a true belief system. In any case, the teachings of Shinran played a role in converting leftists. However, I don't think your typical adherent was thinking such sophisticated thoughts—they were just grateful for his teachings. So in the Meiji period, I think they played almost no role…

Fukuzawa Yukichi (1835–1901) was a follower, which is interesting because not many samurai were. Quite a few prosperous farmers bought their sons a position as a samurai. I hear it happened in my own family. When that happened, they would leave Jōdo Shinshū and convert to Jōdo Buddhism. They had to, because the domain had no interest in someone who might be more loyal to their sect than to the domain's lord, much like Communist parties demanded allegiance to their Central Committee. So Fukuzawa's sticking with Jōdo Shinshū was unusual. His house was right across the street from a Jōdo Shinshū temple. When he returned from his trip to America, he began to think that it was the ideals of freedom and human rights in America and

Europe that led to the rise of these regions.

Also, as someone living in the early Meiji period, Fukuzawa was surprised by the American practice of giving speeches—of oral transmission of information to the masses. Incorporating this custom into Japanese culture led to the creation of the lecture hall in Mita [Tokyo]. I don't think the tradition of addressing the masses really existed before the Meiji period. Fukuzawa probably recognized some trace of that custom in the way that Jōdo Shinshū monks delivered sermons, and figured that was enough to build on. He used the Mita lecture hall as his main venue for delivering speeches to students in order to spread his ideas.

Incidentally, the sermons delivered by Jōdo Shinshū temple monks are a little bit strange—rhythmical, like a song.

Japanese Suffering

Keene   I'm not sure how well Chikamatsu's dramas reflect the society of his time, but, if we can trust his writings, Buddhism wasn't a very big deal for the Japanese back then. It was just the idea that when you die you'll move on to paradise, or be reborn on the same lotus flower, and that became an excuse for young men and women to die together. It was probably a sort of consolation—if we can't be together in this world, they figured, we'll be together in the next. It's very hard to say exactly what Chikamatsu himself believed, though.

Taking his *Meido no hikyaku* [The Courier for Hell] as an example, in the end Chūbei and Umegawa run away together. Thinking that they've made a clean escape, Chūbei's father gives thanks to Amitābha, but ironically the two are soon arrested. A straight reading of that would imply that Chikamatsu did not believe in Amitābha. In *Shinjū kasane izutsu* [The Love Suicide at Double-ringed Well] too, in the end Tokubei and Ofusa die together. But in fact, Tokubei followed the Jōdo sect of Buddhism, while Ofusa followed Nichiren. It wouldn't do for them to wind up in different paradises—they had to belong to the same sect. So they both decide to follow Nichiren so that they can go to paradise together, but that somehow feels like cheating. [Laughs] His *Shinjū mannensō* [The Love Suicides in the Women's Temple] has nothing good to say about Shingon Buddhism. In all, one can only believe that Chikamatsu didn't put much stock in Buddhism.

Shiba   In Europe, the various native faiths that predated Christianity have stuck around as secondary Christian artifacts, like Halloween in Ireland and Santa Claus in America, thereby drawing more followers to the Catholic church. But theologians don't believe in such things, and they've spent millennia making arguments about the existence of—and proof of—God, finally resulting in the development of the great ideas that established Europe.

So this giant lie about the absolute may have enabled the rise of Europe, but Japan was a relativistic world where people only believed what they saw with their own eyes. The Meiji Restoration sent Japan in the philosophical direction of Europe. We mostly wear Western clothes now, so I guess we consider ourselves at least one percent European, but we're very different in terms of our culture and literature. Not that I'm trying to say there's anything unique about Japanese culture or literature.

It's very hard to be Japanese. Trying to say that's a good thing about Japanese culture would just be narcissism. But on the other hand, denying Japanese culture would be a denial of our very existence. It would be going too far to call that the tragedy of the Japanese, but I'm sometimes jealous when I see followers of Islam, and think of how happy they must be. [Laughs]

Keene   Europeans visiting early Edo Japan judged it to be about as culturally developed as Europe. When I consider things objectively, I think that the level of Japanese culture at the time actually far exceeded that of Europe in all respects.

For those missionaries who claimed it was about the same, however, I suppose they were probably taking into consideration the fact that they had Christianity, even if they didn't have particularly good life-styles. Religion was the most important thing for Europeans of that time, although not necessarily for the Japanese.

For one thing, Europeans were surprised at how clean things were in Japan. In a letter, one missionary wrote that Japanese houses were so clean they didn't know where to spit. I guess spitting was just something you did in European houses. The floors in European eateries were covered in straw to help hide the scraps that people threw away. That or they would feed them to the dogs. So you can imagine how surprised Europeans must have been when they saw Japanese homes. How cultured they must have seemed.

Even so, Europeans viewed the lack of Christianity as an enormous cultural deficiency. Europeans were also troubled when they came into contact with Buddhism, because it was so similar to Christianity. Even the specifics—the incense in the temples, the sound of bells, the *juzu* prayer beads—were eerily similar. One explanation they proposed was that God created Christianity in Europe, while the Devil created Buddhism in Japan. The Devil was originally an angel, after all. By explaining the similarities between Christianity and Buddhism in that way, they were able to justify their religion and their lifestyles.

Japanese Buddhists all supported a particular temple. They had to. Some would visit the Ise shrine to show their respect to Shintō, but they didn't seem to think about religion much in their daily lives. Europeans, up to the nineteenth century at least, were thinking about religion in everything they did.

Shiba   They did indeed. Taking cleanliness as a minor point from among all the things that you mentioned, the history of cleanliness in Europe probably developed with the Protestants, or maybe from German customs, and made its way to America from there. Americans are quite clean themselves, but the Japanese are in a different class.

I had a friend, deceased now, a Korean intellectual and author named Sunwoo Hwi (1922–1986). He used to constantly bug me with questions about why the Japanese are so clean. I in turn asked him why

Koreans aren't. He seemed to believe that the Japanese persecuted Koreans because they didn't consider Koreans to be as clean as they were. He was born in 1922, so he well knew the era of Japanese persecution of Koreans, and that's what he considered to have been the key factor. I tried to explain it away, saying "I don't know, maybe it's just that Japan is so humid and sticky that we have to always be wiping surfaces down." He didn't let me get away with that, though. He'd say, "It's even more humid in Southeast Asia. What makes Japan so different?"

Okinawans are very clean, too. They've been that way for a long time, I don't know why. Shintō doesn't really have any doctrines, but if it did they would be about cleanliness. So I suppose that Japan has been this way since olden times.

People from other Asian countries seem to consider Japan's cleanliness obsession strange, too. I'm sure they wonder why the Japanese are always wiping things down and sweeping and such.

This is just a minor cultural difference, not a deep-rooted problem. That's what you would think, but Japan has Shintō at its core, and part of that is the belief that cleanliness is of utmost importance, something of the greatest reverence. From the perspective of Christianity or Buddhism, Shintō must seem completely devoid of content. It's just all about making things clean. Then along comes Buddhism. The Buddhists do things like, say, they paint temple pillars red like at the Hōryū temple. But when the paint gets old and starts to peel, they just leave it like that. The peeling paint on the pillars in old Japanese temples show a purity resulting from cleansing by wind and frost. The Ise shrine wasn't painted at first, because being unpainted was considered to be cleaner. So it looks like this predilection toward cleanliness started with early-Shintō animism.

Even couples committing suicide in Chikamatsu's jōruri convert to Nichiren Buddhism as a shortcut to purification. They don't experience much ideological suffering in doing so. That's not because the Japanese lack a culture of ideological suffering, but rather because they have no ideals related to the "absolute."

A minute ago, you mentioned something very interesting about Hirata Atsutane. If his thoughts were influenced by Christianity, I have to wonder how he came into contact with it. He wouldn't have interacted with it under the State Shintō of the Meiji period. So it seems that the connection between Hirata's brand of Shintō and Hirata himself was severed.

Keene That's the issue in Shimazaki Tōson's (1872–1943) *Yoake mae* [Before the Dawn].

Shiba It is, isn't it. That reminds me—in the late Edo period, Hirata-style *kokugaku* [nativist studies] resulted in salons that were patronized by village leaders and wealthy merchants. At these salons, people would recite poetry and all kinds of things. Much like *Before the Dawn*'s protagonist Aoyama Hanzō, Shimazaki Tōson's father studied Hirata kokugaku, and had high status in his farming village. That's not something the warrior class really did. Village leaders and wealthy towns-folk, people like Shiraishi Shōichirō (1812–1880) of Shimonoseki, and sponsors of Chōshū revolutionaries followed Hirata kokugaku, and wrote some very nice poetry. But there's no indication that the Chōshū domain leaders followed Hirata kokugaku.

When the Meiji government formed, they figured they should share a bit of the Restoration with the Hirata kokugaku folks, so the Department of Divinities was created in the Great Council of State, and they were all shoved into there. Having little else to do, they started the anti-Buddhist movement.

European states were built up with Christianity as a base, so no doubt the Meiji government wanted to position Shintō in the same way. Nations need a kind of buttressing—you can't just plop down a bunch of government buildings with no ideological support, so the Japanese at the time must have thought they could use State Shintō just like Europe and America used Christianity.

Meiji-period State Shintō didn't include the strange gods of the *inshi* "immoral shrines" of Edo-period Shintō. Instead there was an assortment of gods from the *Records of Ancient Matters* and *Nihon shoki* [The Chronicles of Japan]. But still there was no ideological system behind it, so honji suijaku saved the gods, but it also made them separate and independent and into the buttressing supporting a nation state, like Christianity.

I wouldn't go so far as to call State Shintō damaging. Even in our time, nobody really believes in Shintō. If someone turning twenty eight decades after the Meiji period began doesn't believe in it, it can't have had that much of an impact. But in any case, the most important thing was for State Shintō to play the role of Christianity. To that end, they had to sever ties with Hirata kokugaku. That was the philosophy of an individual, so it wasn't a solid enough base.

The Shah of Iran thought that he could modernize his country without any buttressing, but Khomeini knew better. He knew that Islam was needed to support the Iranian state, and that's why he was able to drive out the Shah. I'm sure he realized that modernizing was beside the point—religious support was what was important. I'm not a big fan of Khomeini, but I can see how someone creating a new nation would think that way. Setting aside Europe and America, people who want to build modern nations need buttressing.

CHAPTER 7
Japan as a Member of the Global Community

Between Curiosity and Indifference

Shiba The fall of the Berlin Wall was a dramatic global turning point, but in hindsight—and I say this not as a criticism, but as an observation on the Japanese people—isn't it strange that so few Japanese who supported East Germany and the Soviet Union have admitted the error of their ways? [Laughs]

They don't even seem upset about how things turned out. Every day of the year, they sleep, and dream, and wake up, and start a new day, just the same as always. When I see that indifference, I can't help but feel that these people weren't thinking and acting with responsibility, not really—that it was all just talk, just fantasy. If you're just going to dream, you might as well keep on dreaming. The Japanese Communist Party didn't even change its name. Normally you'd think they would be in an uproar trying to rebrand themselves, but no. I guess they figure that Japan is so isolated it doesn't matter, or that it's some kind of Japan-versus-the-world thing. Or maybe that no matter how much the world changes, it doesn't affect Japan. I really couldn't say, despite having watched the situation closely.

Keene It is odd, isn't it. So far as I know, no one has come out and admitted that they read the situation incorrectly, or were mistaken. The Berlin Wall was supposedly constructed to prevent Western spies from getting into East Berlin. Not to prevent people from the East escaping to the West, mind you, but to keep out the Western bad guys. Right. [Laughs]

Shiba Just five or six years ago, a properly elected politician from a major party said that Japan should imitate East Germany, which is crazy enough, but it also makes me wonder if Japan isn't still in a period of isolationism. [Laughs] I really think that sometimes. How do you feel about Japan, on your occasional visits back?

Keene It's been almost forty years since I first lived in Japan, so yes, the country has definitely changed. But there's one thing that hasn't, namely the way that Westerners are viewed.

I'm staying at the Kyoto Hotel tonight. It's a wonderful hotel, but for example while Japanese patrons are provided with a newspaper in their room, there wasn't one in mine. I suppose they figure there's no point in wasting a newspaper on a Westerner, who obviously can't read Japanese, so I never get one. [Laughs] It's like an unshakable belief. Just this morning, they were handing out some kind of questionnaire in Tokyo station, but I wasn't offered one, even when I held my hand out. [Laughs] Again, they didn't want to waste one, I suppose. Westerners are treated almost like monsters—like something that looks human, but isn't really.

I have people approach me speaking English, even right after I've given a presentation in Japanese. Just recently there was an open-air noh performance in Takasaki, Gunma prefecture, and before it began I gave a presentation about noh. Afterwards, former prime minister Nakasone invited me to come speak with him. I'd met him before in a televised interview, but even so he spoke to me in English, as if he assumed I didn't speak Japanese. This was right after an hour-long lecture, mind you, and after having conversation in the past. Even with all that, he seemed to believe I couldn't speak Japanese.

Shiba I'm sure there's a lot of that, and I think it's part of the inferiority complex that Japanese people have about learning English. We study English from junior high school through college, but we're still not very good at it.

I graduated from a language school, which I recently visited on an errand. Unlike when I was there, they now have a modern language laboratory, with systems to help you correct your pronunciation. I saw students using them to study languages like Indonesian and Thai, but never English. People studying English don't want to be seen doing that, because they're embarrassed to show how bad they are at it, despite having studied it since junior high. A Japanese studying Mongolian or Russian or what have you is doing so for the first time in their life, so there's no shame in making mistakes, but that's not the case with English. I think that's a big problem.

It might seem that we're straying from the topic at hand here, but we aren't really. If the Japanese learned, say, Korean starting in junior high, then I think we would conversely feel closer to English. If that were the case, I think you would have gotten your questionnaire.

It might seem like we've made great progress, but for example I think most people in other countries consider the fall of the Berlin Wall something that concerns them. The Japanese, however, see videos of things happening in Europe, and they assume that the German they're hearing is English, which makes it something related to the English-speaking world, something out of a textbook. They watch these things like they're reading a school textbook. This issue is directly related to the way people wonder whether they should vote for, say, the Social Democratic Party of Japan in the next election, but treat it like something happening in a different world, or on another planet even, to exaggerate a bit. Sometimes I can't help but think that in some ways we're still stuck in the Edo period. I'm joking when I blame our English education for it, but still…

Keene There weren't many, but some scholars in Edo Japan did study the West. They got to where they could read Dutch quite well, and I'm sure they studied very hard. In a way, learning Dutch was a way for them to discover the world. They could only do that by learning Dutch.

There's a similar phenomenon today in China, which is undergoing a boom in Japanese studies. There are Japanese schools now, where the Chinese go to learn the language. This is an interesting phenomenon, considering how people there used to view Japanese. Namely, long ago the Chinese considered Japanese to be some odd dialect, not worth learning. But today they do it quite well. For some Chinese, it's their only escape. Mastering Japanese might provide a way to go to Japan. In any case, it's a way to escape the dead end they find themselves in now. There's probably something similar going on with English. The Japanese of long ago didn't have good dictionaries or grammar references, let alone many chances to meet a Dutch person. So I suspect there was a similar kind of psychology behind all the effort they spent learning Dutch.

Today, most Japanese study English with an eye toward what their schools require, or what will be on college entrance exams. They don't necessarily want to learn the language, but if they don't, they can't get into college. That wasn't the case for Japanese of the Meiji period. Some people were amazing English speakers back then. Okakura Tenshin (1862–1913) writes beautifully in English, and reading Natsume Sōseki's English is quite surprising. They of course don't make any grammatical mistakes, but beyond that they just write lovely English. That's the result of really wanting to learn the language. It's very different from today. Of course, there are people with an equal desire even today, but there aren't many, as in the case of most any society.

Shiba   Right. Katsu Kaishū (1823–1899) was born into a family that wasn't quite a retainer to the shogun, and learning Dutch was his only way to escape from his circumstances, so he studied very hard.

Speaking of Katsu Kaishū reminds me of Rembrandt's *The Night Watch*, a painting that I have long loved almost obsessively. Holland has traditionally had a strong civil society, one where merchants become soldiers to protect their towns. When Rembrandt painted *The Night Watch*, however, the Spanish occupiers were gone, and from what I understand these "night watches" were more like social clubs, a form of entertainment. I also understand that the Dutch were big on splitting the bill, so I would imagine it was common for people not to have their individual portrait painted, but instead to commission a group portrait and share the cost.

I visited the Netherlands last year, including the town of Hoorn, which came up at the beginning of our talk today. When I was there I found a museum in a building that used to belong to the Dutch East India Company. Inside were lots of paintings similar to *The Night Watch*. All the people in them strike similar poses, holding muskets or spears. I figured it was a template that had been around for a long time, and that Rembrandt was asked to follow that style. I saw even more of these paintings when I visited a historical museum in town. Holland has the world's oldest civil society, and these paintings really reinforced that impression in me.

We also mentioned the journal of Kattendijke (1816–1866), which is quite different from Katsu Kaishū's. He relates a conversation with a rich merchant in Nagasaki, to whom he says "Nagasaki is a very quiet town, but a single warship from a big country like England could just sail in and take the place over. What would you do if that happened?" The merchant replies, "Worrying about things like that is the shogun's job, not ours." Kattendijke was from Holland, where citizens organized themselves into groups like the peacekeepers in *The Night Watch*, so he was surprised by the lack of national identity revealed in the phrase "that's the shogun's job."

I imagine Kattendijke must have spoken about this with Katsu Kaishū. I also like to imagine that these conversations made Katsu think that establishing a "civil nation" like Holland was key to solving Japan's problems. Eventually Japan did become a civil nation, but in the American mold. That at least allowed people to attain a normal status from lower positions, and solved various other problems. I think that later on, when the shogunate let Katsu decide whether to protect Edo or submit to domestic anti-shogunate forces, these conversations with Kattendijke may have influenced his decision to surrender the city entirely.

Some shogunate retainers later criticized Katsu for how he handled the situation, but he never gave any indication of regretting his decision. He probably considered himself the father of a new civic nation. Not that it arose right away, but he must have foreseen that eventuality—possibly with excessive confidence—when he surrendered Edo. He believed his actions would ensure the birth of a new government. I can't help but wonder if his nightly conversations with Kattendijke might have given rise to that belief. Not that any such conversations are recorded anywhere.

So anyway, when I recently took another look at Rembrandt's paintings, they were just as wonderful as I remembered. From what I understand, the models in *The Night Watch* were supposed to pay one hundred guilders each—they were splitting the bill to pay Rembrandt to paint their portrait. But he didn't paint the picture in quite the way they expected, like a group photo, so in the end they refused to pay him, causing Rembrandt to go broke. Prior to that, though, everyone always paid up. Coming from such a society a nineteenth-century person like Kattendijke must have been surprised when he saw Japanese society, where the merchants were just merchants with no responsibilities toward the state. Surely, he must have said something to Katsu about how strange that seemed. Not that he would have hammered on that issue, being a Dutch gentleman of the time. The Dutch aren't exactly political agitators, so I imagine that he would have brought it up in the natural course of conversation.

Keene   Speaking of Rembrandt, there was a painting in Edo-period Japan that was supposedly done by him. I'm sure it was a forgery, since its motif was the moon, or maybe trees or something. In any case, it shows that the Japanese of the Edo period had heard of Rembrandt. I have no idea how many Dutch paintings made their way to Japan, but those that did were mostly still lifes of flowers arranged in a style very unlike Japanese ikebana. Of course, there was no photography at the time, so the extreme realism of these Dutch paintings was very impressive—unlike with Oriental paintings, standing in front of one of them was like standing in front of an actual flower. I think those Dutch paintings had quite an impact.

One difference was the use of perspective. This was Japan's first contact with perspective in art, and the technique gathered numerous devotees. You started seeing people like Maruyama Ōkyo (1733–1795) and Katsushika Hokusai (1760–1849) using perspective. Of course, they didn't abandon Japanese traditions, but I do believe that the Japanese of that time were starved for stimulation from overseas. The Kanō school was defunct, and nothing much was happening in the domestic art world, so seeing these foreign pictures of people and scenery made artists want to try something similar on their own. Shiba Kōkan (1747–1818) is one interesting example, as is Hiraga Gennai (1728–1780). I think that feeling of "I want to try that, too" is characteristically Japanese.

In today's Japan, for example, there's no sport that nobody plays. Take any sport from around the world, and at least some Japanese will be really into it. Dance is that way too—all forms of dance exist in Japan, with at least a few people highly interested in each one. Long ago, the Japanese couldn't travel to other countries, or at least doing so was far more difficult than it is today. Even so, you see people like the daimyo of the Kubota domain painting European-style pictures, with foregrounds and backgrounds.

As far as I know, this only happened in Japan. I've never heard of Indians copying British painting methods, and while there were Italians like Giuseppe Castiglione (1688–1766) painting in China under the Qianlong Emperor, Chinese painters didn't copy him. But Japan's closed borders only increased the desire for stimulus, for new things from the outside. If Westerners had been allowed free access into Japan, the Japanese may have been less interested in them. In short, the Japanese wanted to try the things that their lack of freedom made difficult.

Shiba   I'm like that myself. I thought about giving aerobics a try, so I went to check it out. [Laughs] Turns out it wasn't the thing for me, but I suppose that initial feeling of giving it a shot might be something left over from the Edo period.

In the September 1989 issue of *Chūō kōron*, Miyazaki Ichisada

(1901–1995) told the story of some students who were dispatched from Qing dynasty China to study oil painting in France in the late nineteenth or early twentieth century. They all returned home saying that they could never paint in such a vulgar style. In other words, the Chinese thought that painting was supposed to demonstrate an ideal that lies within one's heart. When asked to paint something as mundane as an apple, they were disgusted and hurried home.

In contrast, the Japanese are perhaps too eager to adopt. You can find all kinds of dance here, from flamenco to Arabian dancing. But still, this enormous Japanese curiosity does not seem to extend to international affairs.

Keene   I think those things have always been quite separate. When the hula-hoop became popular overseas it was just as popular here, but I don't think many Chinese did it. Japanese want to try anything foreign. With food, for example, the Japanese try to outdo the French in cooking. Yet they aren't all that interested in what daily life is like in those countries.

To take a somewhat strange example, over half of the Western Japan researchers I know have Japanese spouses. On the other hand, very few of the Japanese English teachers I know have married English speakers. That makes me think that the Japanese consider matters of the head and heart as separate issues. They're drawn in different directions.

Westerners and the Japanese

Shiba   I met Inoue Yasushi (1907–1991) just a year and a half before he died, and he said a curious thing—that it's about time for the Japanese—or maybe he said Japan—to become a member of the world union. I like that expression, "joining the world union." Not like a labor union, but a union of, like, public bath houses or precious metal dealers or pawn shops.

Edo-period Japan was a closed country, and Meiji-period Japan considered itself weak. Back then we saw ourselves as not quite ready to sit at the table, because we were still learning Western European ways. Winning the Russo-Japanese war made us a bit overbearing, though, and we started to think of ourselves as one of the five great powers. Once the Shōwa period began we needed modernized armed forces, meaning warships and tanks and such. That's a hard thing to do for a country with no oil, and so began the fiction that we're a strong country, a country of the gods. So from the Edo period up until today, we've never really been members in this "world union" that Inoue talked about. We even left the League of Nations, and following the Second World War we were an occupied country. Then after our period of rapid economic growth, we started showering the world with "Made in Japan" products.

Denmark makes furniture, so when the French make furniture they try not to make it in a Danish style, to avoid stepping on the toes of Danish manufacturers. In Europe and America, too, you see this kind of separation of habitats, to use the words of the ecologist Imanishi Kinji (1902–1992). Japan never did that. That's why we've never been members of the world union.

There's danger in interpreting Inoue's phrase too broadly, but my own take is that even after the Edo period, we never joined the world union. Even if we've sometimes been a pro tem member, or a quasi-member, or an apprentice member, we've never been a full member. Members have duties and responsibilities, and we've finally reached the era where Japan needs to step up.

I was very moved when the Berlin Wall came down. It was this huge historical event—bigger even than Mao's rise to power—and it was happening during my own lifetime. Anyone who can view something like that as a mere news item on TV with no impact on their own life can't be thinking of him or herself as a member of a world union. But that attitude is still around, even today.

Keene   I think it's an after-effect of Japan's period as a closed nation.

Shiba   An after-effect indeed.

Keene   Specifically, it's the idea that Japan can import things from other countries and copy things that other countries are doing, but that Japan is nonetheless fundamentally different from those countries.

During the Edo period, teaching Japanese to foreigners, and even to the Ainu, was forbidden. That ensured that anything written in Japanese could only be read by Japanese people. The idea was that if non-Japanese were able to read and write just like the Japanese did, then Japan's secrets might leak to the outside world.

So "Westerners can't read Japanese" was the status quo then, and a lot of people think the situation is the same today. I've been studying Japanese for forty-some-odd years, but even after Japanese people see me give a speech in Japanese, some assume that I can't read the language. They're surprised when they find out that I can, and even more surprised when I write even the simplest thing.

It's like Westerners who have worked their way within the castle walls of Japan are a foreign body within Japanese society, and cause a certain discomfort. Even today, there's a sense that Japan exists in a different dimension from other countries. So even if the Japanese acknowledge on the surface that they are members of global society, they don't actually recognize it in their daily lives, and they don't feel that it's true.

Shiba   That does seem to be the case. I was very impressed when I learned that half of the residents in Amsterdam are foreigners, many of them from Southeast Asia, Africa, and other parts of the developing world. But they're all given equal rights. They're all considered Dutch. There's no prejudice, not just on the surface, but even below the surface. Well, I don't know what lies at the very bottom, but I certainly saw nothing that looked like prejudice.

Even the foreign employees of Japanese companies, who can do quite well there, are given the same rights as Dutch citizens after they've lived there for two years. If their kids go to college there they'll receive financial aid, and when they're younger the parents receive support payments. It's all so fair that it makes me wonder if it isn't *too* fair. After living there for a few years, residents can even vote in city elections for mayor or whatever. Everyone considers that to be natural. They don't see it as something wonderful about the Netherlands, but rather think that's the way the world should be. After seeing Amsterdam, it's hard to believe that Tokyo and Osaka aren't run the same way.

Keene I saw something similar in Italy. In Italian towns—big cities like Rome and Milan especially—Africans were selling things on the streets, though I doubt they had any special kind of visa when they entered the country. I figured that this must bother the native Italians, so I asked a friend about it, but he said he didn't mind. Until fairly recently many Italians would head overseas to North or South America, and he said that now it was their turn to welcome foreigners. Since Italy was once a major source of emigration, it was only natural for it to become a destination for immigrants. I found that attitude to be quite admirable.

Shiba An excellent attitude indeed. The person who explained the situation to me in Amsterdam did so simply so that I would understand. In elementary and junior high school courses, they aren't scared into avoiding prejudice against foreigners because of what might happen in the future, when foreigners outnumber natives, for example that the country would be destroyed or what have you. They're just taught that everyone is equally Dutch, and that's the best way to be.

As someone from Japan, a country that may or may not be a member of the world community, this was the simple explanation I was given. I think it offers some good ideas for Japan's own future, and we need to consider them seriously. Bringing the world into Japan and engaging more with other countries won't be the end of the Japanese people and culture. Instead, it will make us stronger as a country.

Afterword, by Shiba Ryōtarō

The word *natsukashii* [nostalgic] has been in the Japanese language since ancient times.

However, in the era that Donald Keene studies, the eleventh-century world of *Genji monogatari* [The Tale of Genji], that word didn't refer to reflections on the past, but simply to a longing of the heart; it took on its modern meaning sometime after Japan's medieval period. *Kokusen'ya kassen* [The Battles of Coxinga], one of the Chikamatsu *jōruri* that Keene so fervently translated when he was young, uses *natsukashii* in the line "Oh, how I long for Japan!" so it clearly carried that meaning by the time the play was written in 1715.

Sitting down and speaking with Keene was *natsukashii* in the modern sense. There is no one else who makes me feel quite the way that he does. When he sits across from you at the table, he brings a comity that puts you at ease, thereby avoiding any feeling of heaviness.

Perhaps like many literary scholars, he is attracted to fine linguistic expressions, in any tongue. Such expressions preferably contain multiple layers of meaning, and furthermore sound beautiful. That language can be written on paper or spoken on a stage, since Keene is of course a theater devotee of the first degree. From a young age his research has moved back and forth between the art of letters and that of speech.

During the conversation that became this book, Keene brought up the example of Chikamatsu's *Meido no hikyaku* [The Courier for Hell], in the context of how literature can convey humanity. In that story, the hot-headed Chūbei foolishly steals three hundred pieces of gold. This is an act that can only lead to his death, but the characters have a humanity that makes the audience feel they, too, might do the same thing under certain circumstances, and are thus touched by the author from beyond time and space.

After that, the conversation naturally moved to Shakespeare's *Julius Caesar*. Speaking to Mark Antony, Caesar says that he wants only fat men near him, not those who have grown thin reading books. After that—and here is where the humanity is—Caesar turns to Mark Antony and says "Come on my right hand, for this ear is deaf." It is lines like this that make Caesar come to life on the stage.

When Keene was young, he read Zeami's *Matsukaze* [Wind in the Pines]. In his *Nihon bungaku no naka e* [Diving into Japanese Literature], Keene writes, "I believe that *Wind in the Pines* is one of the greatest works of literature," and adds:

> Some may think me strange for saying so, but I feel that the best Japanese poetry isn't *waka* or *renga* or haiku, but *yōkyoku*, the poetry of noh chants. Yōkyoku is the poetry that best expresses the functionality of Japanese. Among the more than two hundred such poems that exist, I think *Wind in the Pines* is the best of them all. I'm moved every time I read it.
>
> I'm not the only one. Since starting to teach at Columbia University I've read *Wind in the Pines* seven or eight times with my students, and none have failed to feel as I do. Each one has said it makes them glad they learned Japanese. I don't think it is possible to fully convey that work in translation, no matter how skillful the translator. It is impossible to capture the rhythm of the sounds. *Wind in the Pines* is thus indeed a perfect work of literature.

Reading literature is an experience that takes place at the deepest levels of the spirit. I can't help but wonder how many people have experienced *Wind in the Pines* in that way in Japanese.

It was years before Keene was able to view *Wind in the Pines* as a noh drama. He finally did at a performance in 1953 in Osaka, and while he says he enjoyed watching Kita Roppeita's (1874–1971) *Sagi* [The Heron], the main attraction, *Wind in the Pines,* was a disappointment. Keene attributes this to a replacement for the lead role due to the sudden death of Noguchi Kanesuke (1879–1953), but I get the impression that his deep reading of the work left him with a mental image more brilliant and profound than the actuality of the stage. He says the music in that image was more like Debussy than the drums and flutes of traditional Japanese theater.

Of course, Keene's interests are not limited to literary scholarship. He has also studied Honda Toshiaki (1744–1820), the late-Edo mathematician and statesman whose ideals exceeded the reality of the shogunate. He is also deeply insightful about many other aspects of Japan, from the Confucianism, *kokugaku* [nativist studies], Buddhism, and Western studies of the Edo period to the letters and diaries of soldiers during the Pacific War.

When I speak with Keene and listen to his voice, I'm unsurprised to hear the sound of the wind in pines in distant Sumanoura. Alongside that I hear the wails of the sisters in *Wind in the Pines*, and I start to feel nostalgic for Keene, even as he sits right before me. I hope that our readers will understand why that might be.

About the Authors

Donald Keene

Donald Keene was born in New York in 1922. He graduated from Columbia University in 1942 and immediately entered the Navy Japanese Language School. He served as a translator and interpreter during World War II. Afterwards, he obtained a doctoral degree from Columbia. He first taught at Cambridge University in 1948–53. He spent 1953–55 at Kyoto University, then became a professor at Columbia in 1955. Since then, he has published over 50 books related to Japan's literature and culture in Japanese and English. He received Japan's Order of Culture in 2008.

Shiba Ryōtarō

Shiba Ryōtarō was born in Osaka in 1923, and graduated from the Mongolian department at the Osaka Foreign Language School. In 1960, while working as a newspaper reporter, he received the Naoki Prize for his first novel *Fukurō no shiro* (Castle of Owls), after which he became a full-time novelist. He has received many other awards, including the Japan Art Academy's Imperial Award, for his many historical works such as *Kūkai no fūkei* (Kūkai the Universal: Scenes from his Life). He received the Order of Culture in 1993. Other main works include *Ryōma ga yuku* (Ryōma Goes his Way), *Kaidō o yuku* (On the Highway), *Kono kuni no katachi* (The Form of Our Country), and *Saka no ue no kumo* (Clouds above the Hill: A Historical Novel of the Russo-Japanese War). He died in February 1996.

Index

（英文版）世界のなかの日本　十六世紀まで遡って見る
（『ドナルド・キーン著作集 第九巻 世界のなかの日本文化』所収）
Edo Japan Encounters the World: Conversations Between Donald Keene and Shiba Ryōtarō

2018 年 3 月 27 日　　第 1 刷発行

著　者　ドナルド・キーン
　　　　司馬遼太郎
訳　者　トニー・ゴンザレス
発行所　一般財団法人出版文化産業振興財団
　　　　〒 101-0051　東京都千代田区神田神保町 3-12-3
　　　　電話　03-5211-7282（代）
　　　　ホームページ　http://www.jpic.or.jp/

印刷・製本所　大日本印刷株式会社

定価はカバーに表示してあります。
本書の無断複写（コピー）、転載は著作権法の例外を除き、禁じられています。

© 1992, 1996, 2013 by Donald Keene, Uemura Yōkō and Shiba Ryōtarō Memorial Foundation
Printed in Japan
ISBN 978-4-86658-018-0